Bridal Moments

A SURVIVAL GUIDE
TO WEDDING CHAOS

Helen Dugdale

with Brendan Moffett

Marshall Cavendish
Editions

395.22

Copyright © 2009 Swell Ideas Ltd

First published in 2009 by

Marshall Cavendish Limited
Fifth Floor
32–38 Saffron Hill
London ECIN 8FH
United Kingdom
T +44 (0)20 7421 8120
F +44 (0)20 7421 8121
sales@marshallcavendish.co.uk
www.marshallcavendish.co.uk

A CIP record for this book is available
from the British Library

ISBN 978-1-904879-90-9

Designed by www.stazikerjones.co.uk

Printed and bound in Great Britain
by TJ International Ltd, Padstow, Cornwall

To my family

CONTENTS

BRIDAL MOMENTS – A SPOT OF LIGHT RELIEF WHEN YOU'RE HEAD-DEEP IN WEDDING CHAOS

B ridal moments – we all have them. From the second he utters those little words, to the minute your last wedding gift is unwrapped. The transition from bride-to-be to full-blown bride is a helter-skelter journey, filled with love, laughter and the odd black hole waiting for you to fall into. Each moment should be treasured, so you can revel, rejoice or squirm in years to come.

This book offers some well-worn pearls of wisdom, shares stories of other people's bridal moments – good, bad and ugly – and will provide you with a spot of light relief when you're head-deep in total wedding chaos.

Bridal Moments will help point out the things that will keep you awake at night, mishaps that will have you nibbling on your French-polished nails, and issues that could cause you to squabble with your newly-crowned fiancé.

Think of *Bridal Moments* as the book to read in the bath with a cup of tea and a biscuit. It's the place to turn when you want to laugh at other bridal mishaps, find out what's going on inside your fella's mind and need some sound advice from the brides who have walked down the road to 'I do' before you.

Enjoy all the planning, the power and most of all savour those bridal moments!

The first moment

yes!

THE TROUBLE WITH SOME

WOMEN IS THAT THEY GET

ALL EXCITED ABOUT NOTHING,

AND THEN MARRY HIM.

Cher

Greetings! Whoever you are, whatever your situation: welcome to the long wiggly road to a magnificent marriage.

Congratulations on your engagement – there is no better time or reason to spend copious amounts of money.

While you're planning your big day and basking in your newfound bride-to-be fame, you'll experience many magical moments, all of which should be relished and remembered. It can be an emotional rollercoaster and along the way there will be some hilarious times and no doubt the odd hair-raising experience. But, each one is part of your unique journey to saying 'I do'.

Bridal Moments is filled with sparkly gems of guidance dating back to the very first wedding that took place, to some modern trinkets that we've stolen from recent brides. There are tips on how to get your husband-to-be to pull his weight, advice on how to stay calm and composed, and lots of fascinating wedding facts with which to bore your unmarried mates. There are also wedding stories that will make your toes curl and see you rejoicing that they didn't happen to you.

This isn't the place for all the usual doyley-chatter that you can get from the glossy magazines. It's just simple, straight-talk about weddings.

So let's get started with a blooming good moan.

Was it a decent proposal?

So how did he (or you) pop that big question: at the top of the Eiffel Tower or the Empire State Building? While walking on the beach, in a swanky restaurant, or maybe during a picnic in the park? Was it what you'd expected? How you've always dreamt it would be? Admit it, we've all spent a sly five minutes (if not hours) pondering on the proposal. That moment when the world stops spinning, adorable Walt Disney bunnies pop up from behind the nearest lettuce, and cute cupids fly overhead blowing big smackers in your direction.

But, while you're sat all coy and smug on your leather sofa dreaming of the moment, how do you think the blokes feel? They've got the pressure of knowing how important the occasion is, and how vital it is for both your future happiness that there are no screw-ups. Those few sacred seconds when the words are muttered are meant to be encased in silk, and will form the ultimate love story over which your great-grandchildren will swoon. The men know all too well that if they mess it up, they will never hear the end of it. The so-called love story will become the mortifying tale that's loaded into a gun and fired into their face, whenever a perfect take the mickey moment rolls up.

When it goes wrong

Research in the USA showed a whopping 85 percent of females are disappointed in the way their partners proposed. A recent Bridal Moments survey asking the same question, showed 72 percent had the hump about the way it happened. Were you disappointed?

I have to admit my own experience wasn't what I'd expected or dreamed. I'm not the kind of girl that spent years dreaming of her big day. For years I even struggled with the reasons for actually getting married. Then I met Mr Right and he slowly started to change my mind. After daring to give my perfect proposal some thought, I started to dream he'd pop the question somewhere hot, and while I was looking fantastic in an expensive dress with matching heels and handbag. But it wasn't to be. The proposal took place while we were travelling, and neither heels nor hand-bag were in sight. Three months into our four-month trip and he still hadn't asked, I was beginning to get impatient. We'd visited some magnificent places, where I thought on many occasions the words were on the tip of his furry tongue. Bikini-clad on the golden sandy beaches in Hawaii, watching the sunset over Ayers Rock, fumbling in a hammock in Fiji, traipsing after the Incas in Peru, getting drunk on vino tinto in Argentina or tangoing in Buenos Aires. All these magical places just kept whizzing by with no sound of those little words. There always seemed to be something that wasn't quite right. Whether it was bottom problems in Ayers Rock, itchy mosquito bites in Fiji, altitude sickness in Peru, or too much vino tinto in Argentina. Even dragging him to places called 'Love-Bird Lagoon' and 'Honeymoon Beach' didn't penetrate my enthusiasm into his grey matter. As the days whizzed by, I packed up my thoughts of going home wearing a big sparkly ring and shoved them to the back of my rucksack.

The last stop on our trip was Brazil. It was while we were stood gawping at the wonders of Iguaçu Falls (Foz du Iguaçu) that he finally did it. His timing was impeccable – I couldn't have looked worse. I was sporting a week-old cold sore, greasy hair, mucky jeans and a sarong as a scarf. I looked like a male German exchange-student. But that aside, it was a wonderful time to do it. The waterfall was thundering down in front of us and we were both lapping up the experience.

I took a deep breath and tried to inhale some of the fresh, clear mist that was rising from the waterfall. I rather poetically (pathetically) said, 'This is nature at its best!' A second later, the bloke who back then was just a mere boyfriend, put his arms around me and said, 'No, what would make it nature at its best is if you would marry me. Let's get married!'

In complete amazement, I just repeated the same words over and over. 'Are you serious? Are you serious?' He twirled me and my waterproof mac round and I gave off a really pathetic high-pitched piglet-type squeal. We had a photo taken to capture the moment. It's hardly a shot for the front of next month's *Cosmo Bride* magazine, but it is a romantic memento of a magical moment. Even if we do both look dog-rough.

There was no large diamond ring bought beforehand to mark the momentous occasion, so Brazil's newest fiancé pulled out two rather grubby coins. After that, we returned to our grimy 2-star hotel, drank copious amounts of cheap wine and fell asleep watching *Friends* – the one where Monica and Chandler get married. It was like it was meant to be. It wasn't the love story I'd expected, but it was romantic and has great wind-up value.

When you start digging around it seems there are loads of people who have got an engagement yarn that's worth a snigger.

Carole and Rich, from Melbourne, Australia get a titter whenever they tell their tale. Rich whisked Carole off to a lovely beachfront cabin for a romantic weekend away where he was intending to ask the big question. On the way they stopped at KFC for some greasy snacks. 'We were tucking into our family bucket of food, when my life flashed in front of me,' explains Rich, 'I started to imagine how we'd tell our future children about the story of our engagement and I panicked. I realised I couldn't tell them that we were away at a cabin together, because they'd know we'd had sex before getting married. So instead of proposing on the beach as the sun set, I asked Carole in the KFC car park, while we were surrounded by deep fried chicken. It was pure greasy romance, but at least we've got a clean story to tell the kids!'

Anton, from Leicestershire, thought he had it all sorted when he decided to propose to his girlfriend while on holiday in Hawaii. The table was booked, his tear-jerking speech was in his top pocket and he was confident it would all go smoothly. As they left the hotel all dressed up and ready for a night of Hawaiian love, it started to rain. 'I didn't think anything about the weather. I was looking forward to a few drinks and asking Nadia to be my wife,' said Anton. 'We were early for our dinner reservation so stopped at a bar for a cocktail. By the end of the first cocktail it was raining harder. So we ordered another drink and sat back and watched as it started to bounce off the pavement. As the evening went on we had more cocktails and started to get drunk. After a while I suggested we should go and get something to eat. By that time I had more than enough liquid-courage inside me. But Nadia refused to move. I tried every tactic to get her to leave the bar, but it was no good, she wasn't budging. She didn't want to get her new shoes wet. So I was forced to give up all my plans of a romantic meal and order another cocktail and some chips! By the end of the evening we were both plastered and rolled back to the hotel.' Filled to the brim with Hawaiian cocktails, but still keen to pop the question, Anton decided to ask anyway. 'As I lay on the bed in just my boxer shorts having a scratch, followed by a cocktail-fuelled burp, followed by a rather pathetic, "Will you marry me?" Then without even waiting for a reply, I fell asleep.' Anton continues, 'I sneakily didn't mention it in the morning in case she'd forgotten or hadn't heard me. But within minutes of waking up she took great pleasure in reminding me of my romantic gesture and put me through several hours of ridicule before actually saying yes!'

Female spoilers

However, it's not always the gentlemen that are at fault. I know several ladies that have done their fair share of unpicking the romance. Maria and Owen, from Yorkshire, had been together for several years when they decided it was time to tie the knot. So they booked a romantic weekend in Paris. Unlike most other couples, Maria and Owen were particularly organised; they went shopping together to buy the ring and asked friends to be bridesmaids and ushers, even before the question had been asked! When their well-planned weekend in Paris finally came around they arrived at the airport, where Maria excitedly handed over the passports for inspection. The flight-desk attendant checked Owen's details and handed him back his documents. He then checked Maria's passport, but instead of handing it back and wishing them 'bon voyage', the attendant said there was a problem. 'He kept looking from my passport to my flight confirmation,' explains Maria. 'After a few minutes he said I wasn't going to be able to travel. When I asked why, he informed me that the name on my passport didn't match the name on my flight confirmation. I was dumbfounded. How could my name be different? I tried to protest but he handed back my documents and there staring up at me from my passport was my surname from my first marriage. I'd completely forgotten to change my name after I got divorced. I cried like a baby. All Owen could do was hide his laughter and hug me. Our weekend in Paris, filled with champagne, romance, and my perfectly planned engagement, flew away just like the plane that we should have been on!' Unable to leave the country, but still determined to get engaged, Maria and Owen jumped into the car and drove to Warwickshire, where he finally did the deed outside Warwick Castle. 'When it came to asking the question, Owen was dying for a wee,' laughs Maria. 'He muttered the words, pushed the ring on my finger and disappeared behind the castle wall! It wasn't the Champs-Élysées, and it certainly wasn't the classic romantic proposal that I'd planned for. But I wouldn't change it.'

What would your great-grandmother say?

So are you wrong to be disappointed when the proposal doesn't fit your dreams? Surely you should be satisfied that you've found that special someone and that a ring with a sparkly stone is heading to a finger near you?

In days of old, ladies were just happy to find a suitor and become a Mrs. There was no time or place to moan about how the question was asked. It was just a case of being satisfied you were saved from the ridicule of being a spinster and left on the shelf.

Oh, will Heaven grant I may love and be loved someday. Then I shall be engaged.

Sarah Elizabeth Jewett, from her diary, 1840

Woman's Chance to Marry

1/4 of 1 per cent from 50 to 60 years of age

3/8 of 1 per cent from 45 to 50 years of age

2 1/2 per cent from 40 to 45 years of age

3 3/4 per cent from 35 to 40 years of age

15 1/2 per cent 30 to 35 years of age

18 per cent from 25 to 30 years of age

52 per cent from 20 to 25 years of age

14 1/2 per cent from 15 to 20 years of age

Anon, *Romance of the Zanigs*, 1904

Back then you found a gentleman friend, courted for a while, then he asked your father for your hand in marriage. Your position on the social stepladder had an effect on where the actual proposal took place. For the ladies of a certain social standing, the question might be asked via a poetically handwritten letter from a beau miles away, or during a romantic walk in the grounds of your country manor. While for those on the lower rung, the proposal could easily happen in the parlour of your parents' house, while you're sitting on a hard chair next to a roaring coal fire with your dad's large stained vest and pants hanging overhead and the bedpan filled with wee just a few feet away.

If your engagement story wasn't filled with all the fluffy stuff and sparkle that you'd hoped, fear not. There is still plenty of time to rake back some magic, because from hereon in, what you say goes.

Go forth and use your new bride-to-be power.

It's my day, I'll get my way

HUSBANDS ARE LIKE FIRES.

THEY GO OUT WHEN

UNATTENDED.

Zsa Zsa Gabor

Engaged-to-be-married

This is the bit between getting engaged and getting married, which is imaginatively and traditionally called 'engaged-to-be-married'. In days gone by the engagement period was used to help negotiate a bride-price for the woman's relatives, who were losing a valuable member of their family. Centuries later, the situation was reversed with fathers paying their future son-in-law money to take their daughter. The engagement then became a time to agree the price and to collect the bride-to-be's possessions.

Thankfully none of that archaic nonsense is relevant any more and the engaged couple can now just get on with the enjoyment of planning their wedding day, and figuring out how the hell they're going to pay for it.

Now what?

So your letterbox is probably stuffed to the brim with cards, your mantelpiece is bejewelled with fancy engagement cards and your new fiancé is grinning from ear-to-ear with all the praise and back-slapping. Life is just rosy. Both families are (hopefully!) over the moon with the news, and questions are already starting to flying around: 'When's the big day?', 'What are you going to wear?', 'Can I be bridesmaid?'

It's around this time that you'll both start changing. It's only a slight shift in behaviour and you'll be the first to flip. You'll develop an obsession with wedding magazines. It usually begins with a longing look at the glossies, then a stroke, then a sniff and then finally a purchase. But you can never manage to buy just one. It usually results in you carting home three or four of the blooming things home. After endless days of sitting on your behind, sipping your skinny-chai-latte while flicking through the pages, you'll be fit to burst. Excitement will be escaping out of every orifice and you'll spend the next few weeks drowning in your own bridal saliva and boring the backside off all your single friends, about anything remotely related to the world of weddings.

DID YOU KNOW?

THE AVERAGE AGE OF A
BLUSHING BRIDE IS 32 YEARS
AND SIX MONTHS OLD AND
THE GORGEOUS GROOM IS
35 YEARS AND THREE MONTHS.

THERE WERE 254,400
MARRIAGES IN ENGLAND
AND WALES IN 2002. OF THESE,
150,200 WERE FIRST ARRIAGES
FOR BOTH PARTIES, WHILE
46,700 WERE REMARRIAGES
FOR BOTH PARTIES.

All data taken from The National Statistics Office and reproduced
under the terms of the Click-Use License

Think about it. It's the only day in your entire life when you choose exactly how everything is. From what people eat, to what they wear, and what music they listen to. The power of the bride is just immense and it starts here.

Try this: Stand in the middle of your living room, grab your favourite wedding mag and twirl round with it in your outstretched arms, while screeching your new wedding mantra: 'It's my day, I'll get my way!'

How great does it feel!

While you're busy jumping around with glee, the man that started the wedding cart rolling will also disappear up his back passage, but for a very different reason. The bloke, who was for such a short time excited, romantic, and just generally lovely, will suddenly evaporate. As the mention of the word 'wedding' increases, it's only a matter of time before he turns all 'Great Suprendo' and vanishes. Or even if he doesn't vanish completely, he'll develop fantastic super powers and be able to tap into your thoughts on starting a conversation about the big day, and then scarper before you get chance to utter a word. Even the rustle of an envelope will leave him twitching, as he anticipates having to spend a whole two minutes of his day looking at a brochure for a venue. Apparently, this is just the natural process that the male goes through after he's asked the question. It takes a while to finally sink in that he might actually have to get involved with his own wedding.

Hereon in, all mention of boyfriends, fiancés, grooms or husbands-to-be will be referred to as Lazy Ass.

Wedding sum

Considering it's just one day, weddings are usually very expensive and take up loads of time and effort. We've been doing some wedding sums to show just how much time planning a wedding can take, and how the weight of the organisation is spread between a typical couple. The wedding sum can be used to make Lazy Ass feel guilty about how bone idle he is. It's also the perfect excuse for spending over your budget. After all, you are investing so much of your precious time.

Average time male spends planning wedding	5 hrs
Average time female spends planning wedding	355 hrs
Total time spent planning wedding	360 hrs
Average length of wedding	11 hrs
Average hourly wage for male	£15.26
Average hourly wage for female	£12.16

The Equation:

TPW (time planning wedding) + TAW (time at wedding)
x PC (planner's cost) = Wage bill for wedding

The Sums:

Groom wedding sum:

5 (TPW) + 11 (TAW) x £15.26 (PC) = **£244.16**

Bride wedding sum:

355 (TPW) + 11 (TAW) x £12.16 (PC) = **£4,450.56**

Interesting wedding facts to drop into conversation:

The average cost of a wedding is now £20,000

London is still the most expensive at £22,906 and Northern Ireland is the cheapest at £15,296

Average price of a traditional wedding dress is £826

Average price of a non-traditional wedding dress is £176

The cost of getting married has risen 75 percent since 1998

Data reproduced with kind permission of www.confetti.co.uk

Setting the date – practicalities

The day

Saturday was once the most popular day to get married but, as with most traditions, that has been booted out of the window, and now any day of the week is good to say 'I do'. Friday and Sunday are potentially good days and guests may even take a day off work if they really like you. Avoiding Saturdays can also mean you get discount on venues, caterers and entertainment.

A Good Old Fashioned Rhyme

Monday for wealth
Tuesday for health
Wednesday the best of all
Thursday for crosses
Friday for losses
Saturday for no luck at all.

The month

If you're dribbling over the thought of a sunny service or have set your heart on a handful of hydrangeas, then choose to marry in June, July or August, when the sun just might shine.

Early September, Christmas Day, Valentine's Day, Mother's Day and Easter are also really busy times of the year when venues may be pre-booked and florists are usually flat out.

Also, try to make sure that your date doesn't coincide with your mate's wedding, stag or hen do, the cup final – or most importantly – your period!

Wedding Superstitions

Marry in the month of May, and you'll live to rue the day.
Marry in Lent, you'll live to repent.
......

Married when the year is new, he'll be loving, kind & true,
When February birds do mate, you neither wed nor dread
  your fate.
If you wed when March winds blow, joy and sorrow both
  you'll know.
Marry in April when you can, joy for Maiden and for Man.
Marry in the month of May, and you'll surely rue the day.
Marry when June roses grow, over land and sea you'll go.
Those who in July do wed must labour for their daily bread.
Whoever wed in August be, many a change is sure to see
Marry in September's shrine, your living will be rich
  and fine.
If in October you do marry, love will come but riches tarry.
If you wed in bleak November, only joys will come,
  remember.
When December snows fall fast, marry and true love
  will last.

Anon

Wedding planner or DIY?

Has the exciting thought of using a wedding planner popped into your head yet? It might sound a tad Hollywood, but they don't have to cost a fortune.

Wedding planners, or co-ordinators as they are sometimes known, are really popular Stateside, and more Brits are also opting to use their services.

26 percent of UK couples now employ a wedding planner, compared with 21 percent in 2005.

Rebecca Hulme-Edwardson runs The Wedding and Party Planner. 'Nowadays, people from every walk of life use a wedding planner. It isn't just for the rich and famous. Anyone who is working full-time and has a social life will find it hard to find time to plan their wedding,' she explains. 'On average it can take up to 15 days to plan a wedding. Do you have that much spare time? Using a planner takes the stress out of it all, they can actually save you money and it's someone with an impartial point of view when disagreements arise. On top of this it just sounds great to say you've got a wedding planner!'

You don't even need a million pound budget to pay for a planner. 'Most planners will work with any size budgets. Their costs can start from as little as £2,000–£60,000, depending on exactly what a client needs. Some brides just use a planner to deal with the invites and RSVPs, while others want you to do everything from finding venues, dressing tables, chasing florists, to sending thank you cards and taking things to the dry cleaners. If you're planning a wedding, but pushed for time then a wedding co-ordinator can be a lifesaver.'

Rebecca's top tips for finding a wedding planner:

- Make sure it's someone you get along with. You will be working with this person to plan your big day, so you need to be on the same wavelength.
- Check they have public liability insurance and are a member of the Wedding Alliance.*
- Ask to see a portfolio or testimonials from previous clients.
- Ideally they will have a background in event planning.
- They should be able to pass on savings to you through their industry contacts.

*UK Alliance of Wedding Planners www.ukawp.co.uk

My way or the highway

MARRIAGE IS LIKE A HOT BATH. ONCE YOU GET USED TO IT, IT'S NOT SO HOT.

Anon

It is normal now for the born organisers in your life to start to flock like vultures, desperate to get involved with the preparations. I had to fight off a superbly organised mother and a bossy big sister, both of whom did their utmost to whip me into shape. But, to no avail. When I looked for support from my very own Lazy Ass, he just slithered inside his tortoise shell preparing for full-on wedding hibernation.

I soon realised that planning weddings can actually be a lonely old business. Everyone around you wants to get involved, but when it comes down to it, it's you that has got to make the decisions. Listen out for that gut feeling, let it become your new best friend and it will help you out in times of strife.

Get used to it; organising your wedding is hard work, but lots of fun. You're (hopefully) only going to do it once, so make sure you absorb everything and enjoy every minute. Even the bad bits.

Cinematic Inspiration

Need some light relief? Grab your bridesmaids, a bottle of fizzy and press play on the DVD player. Then sit back and soak up *The Wedding Singer*, *Wedding Crashers* and *Maid in Manhattan* and, of course, what about *My Best Friend's Wedding*?

Balancing the scales

Just how much more will you do than him? We've got the wedding calculator out again and uncovered some serious statistics to show how your 'can-do' attitude versus Lazy Ass's 'won't do' is represented on the wedding scales.

Bride	Groom
Age of average bride: 32	Average age of groom: 35
Average age of female at death: 79 years	Average age of male at death: 75 years
Average hourly wage: £11.92	Average hourly wage: £13.07
If you avoid the divorce courts married for: 47 years	If you avoid the divorce courts married for: 40 years
47 years = 411,720 hours	40 years = 350,400 hours
411,720 X £11.92 = £4,907,702	350,400 X £13.07 = £4,579,728

Make sure all those hours count!

The Budget – the word no bride wants to hear

Yes, budgets are for sensible, reserved, practical, boring souls. But when it comes to weddings, unless daddy has got a forest of money-trees growing on his 100 acres, having an idea of your spend from the off is essential.

According to the website www.confetti.co.uk, the cost of the average traditional wedding in the UK is over £20,000. Talk to any wedding planner and they'll tell you dozens of stories about couples spending way over what they first thought. This is why it's vital you set a budget, now! Wedding guru Rebecca Hulme-Edwardson has convinced many brides to put their money back in their purses. 'It's the smaller budgets that tend to escalate out of control. People say I have a budget of £8,000 and then they proceed to tell me they want a marquee, that they have a guest list of 300 people, and are planning on booking an eight-piece band. It just isn't going to happen. You need to be realistic about what you can get for your money. But just because you've got a smaller budget doesn't mean you can't have a fantastic and unique wedding.'

Rebecca suggests it's advisable to have a budget buffer for those purchases that might just tip it over the edge – 10 percent is the recommended amount. Which means if your budget was £11,000 and you choose to have a contingency of 10 percent, you will need to work to a budget of £9,900, thereby leaving you a contingency sum of £1,100 (£1,100 being 10 percent of £11,000).

**Rebecca's top three things to consider when putting
a budget together:**

1. The number of guests and style of food and
   drink has a tremendous impact on the budget.
   Will you offer a free bar or just provide the
   champagne and wine at the table?
2. Designer wedding dress or off-the-peg? Will
   anyone really see the label? The extra money
   could go towards a swanky honeymoon.
3. Entertainment: a jazz band and singer, followed
   by a DJ will make it a helluva night to remember,
   but cost an absolute fortune. Consider having
   one or the other.

It's so easy to see how budgets can bubble over. The more
research you do into wedding trappings, you start to
discover things that you didn't even know existed and
convince yourself that you need them. How about bespoke
champagne bottles clad in your wedding colours, with your
names and the date of your wedding splattered all over
them? What about a wedding puzzle, where all the questions are related to you and your loved one, for guests to
play with? Novel ideas, but it's really just tat under the all-
that-wedding tinsel.

Christine Northam, a Relate counsellor, has some sound
advice for keeping the cash in the bank. 'Your wedding day
is very special but it's not worth getting into debt for. It's

hard, but try to hold back on your spending. You don't want the weeks after the big day to be spent with your head in your hands surrounded by credit card bills. Owing thousands after the big day will tinge the romance and happy memories – it's just not worth it. Keep a rein on your costs and do your research; get at least two quotes from all suppliers to make sure you get the best deal.'

Local or lavish

These days the possibilities of where you say 'I do' are endless, whereas 20 or 30 years ago tradition was the word on everyone's lips and pleasing the parents was paramount. These days couples usually want to ignore tradition and shout louder than their parents.

When you close your eyes just what it is you see? Golden sandy beaches nestling against a crystal clear sea, an old castle in acres of rugged Scottish countryside, or a hip hotel in the city with champagne and cocktails? Really hard to decide, isn't it?

This is where hours of sitting on your backside scouring wedding magazines and holiday brochures are essential. No matter what Lazy Ass says! Whenever you see anything that sparks a 'gasp', or a 'wow', tear out the page. That way you can show all your clippings to your florist, cake-maker, wedding planner or just your mum, and they'll have a better understanding of just what it is you want.

Need some inspiration?

They say life is a rollercoaster, so why not start married life at the top of one? That's exactly what one couple from the USA did. They took their wedding party on a trip to Playland – a massive amusement park in Vancouver, Canada. Laura Balance, from the park, explains: 'We've had several people propose during the fair, but the most memorable has to be a couple from Louisiana who got married on top of the 75-ft tall hill on the wooden roller-coaster. The minister stood on a catwalk next to the track and the entire wedding party sat in the train. When the minister pronounced them man and wife, we started the coaster. They felt the ride symbolised the ups and downs and twists and turns of marriage!'

If you fancy something a little more down-to-earth, how about the Snowcastle in Kemi, Finland? Marry in the beautiful ice chapel and enjoy a wedding breakfast in the restaurant with its tables made of ice and seats decorated in reindeer fur. If you fancy a beer or glass of champers, then just ask that reindeer walking past with its backpack full of drinks! After you've had your fill, retire to your room and snuggle-up in your sleeping bag. Average temperatures inside the hotel are around 5°C and outside a moderate −30°C. So, it's more warm socks and thermals than lace and skimpy knickers.

Or how about doing it in New York, high heels, big hats and cocktails, champagne and canapés at the Grand Hyatt New York on Park Avenue? What about the top of a snow-covered mountain in Whistler, or on a gondola in the middle of the Grand Canal?

Or, as Tom said in the pub last night, 'I'd like to get married on the moon. That way none of the in-laws will be there.'

Tell them all to shhhhh!

Opinions will be flying at you like bullets. This can be hard if the views are your parents', and they have a financial investment in the wedding. They might really want you to have a church service, but you feel that'd be hypocritical because the last time you stepped foot in a House of God was for weird Uncle Bert's funeral 15 years ago. Or you may want to go abroad but they want to hire the local Labour club. Then there's the guest list. They want all your second cousins from deepest South Wales to come, and you don't want your mates seeing that you have such freaks in your family, and would rather spend the money on some extra bottles of Moët.

Who Should Be Asked to the Wedding?

The parties who ought to be asked are the father and the mother of the gentleman, the brothers and sisters (their wives and husbands also, if married), and indeed the immediate relations and favoured friends of both parties. Old family friends on the bride's side should also receive invitations.

On this occasion the bridegroom has the privilege of asking any friends he may choose to the wedding; but no friend has a right to feel affronted at not being invited, since were all the friends on either side assembled, the wedding breakfast would be an inconveniently crowded reception rather than an impressive ceremonial.

Nugent Robinson, *Collier's* Cyclopedia, 1883

It's not just the people that brought you into the world that can be a pain in the backside. Older siblings, mates and work colleagues also have opinions that get inside your head. What they'd do if they were doing it all over again; how they think you should avoid having a DJ; don't bother with a DVD, you'll never watch it; you really have to have favours. It's hard to figure out what you really want for your day and stay focussed, when you've got dodgy wedding debris floating by from magazines, wedding fairs, friends and just life in general.

How the heck do you stop being so affected by all these schizophrenic voices and ensure that you get the day you really want? Welcome back the calming tones of Christine from Relate. 'It's a well-known fact that getting married is stressful. As much as it's you and your partner's day, those people close to you will naturally be excited and want to get involved. The trick is to let people talk. Let them tell you what they want and what they think you should have. Then let them know their opinions are being taken into consideration,' explains Christine, talking complete sense. 'But then when it comes down to it, it's up to you to get the day you both dreamed of. Just ensure you have the final say.'

Motivating Lazy Ass

TAKE IT FROM ME, MARRIAGE ISN'T A WORD, IT'S A SENTENCE!

Vidor King

Inside the mind of Lazy Ass

Lazy Ass's Wedding Venue Criteria:

- Does the place sell Guinness?
- Is there anywhere I can go for a pint before the ceremony?
- Are there enough lavs?
- Is there a resident bar? I don't want all my mates to sod off at 12.30am and have another party without me and the new wife.
- Quality of female bar staff?
- Do they do good grub/wine?
- Is there somewhere outside to escape from the outlaws?
- Is it cheap?

This is where we peek into the fascinating world of the male mind, so brides can get a better understanding of exactly what goes on in there, if anything. Plus, we also chat with some experts to find out:

Why are blokes so lazy when it comes to planning weddings?

Blokes on blokes:

> *'I start off interested and wanting to have input in to it, but as soon as she gets out that wedding notebook it becomes like a military operation, the can't-be-assed-factor kicks in and the shutters come down.'*
>
> **Lazy Ass on other Lazy Asses**

> *'Men would rather stay out of all the planning, as whatever they say will be quashed by the mother-in-law and bride!'*
>
> **John**

'*Wedding plans are mostly about choosing doyleys,
invitation design and frocks. Things men don't know
about or care about. You can't win – if you don't take
an interest the bride cries. If you do, but disagree with
the bride, she cries. Things invariably end up better
if the man takes no part in the organisation.*'

Anton, Lazy Ass's mate from the rugby club

'*I did bog-all – there were so many more interesting
things happening over the 9–12 months it took to plan
the blooming thing. There was rugby, footy, cricket and
golf to watch and play on any given Saturday when
she wanted me to traipse round wedding venues. Also,
I think it's stupid to sit at home and discuss what drinks
to serve at the reception when you can go down the pub
and do your own research. None of it really interests
blokes and besides, there's usually a mother-in-law
lurking in the shadows – another good reason to
steer clear!*'

Wolfy

The Bridegroom

The groom at a wedding is always secondary in importance to the bride. He generally manages to make his bow, and he always succeeds in carrying off his blushing bride, which is probably all he came for.

Mrs Burton Kingsland,
***Etiquette for All Occasions,* 1901**

What the experts think

I haven't spoken to my mother-in-law for 18 months. I don't like to interrupt her.

Ken Dodd

Maybe there's a psychological reason that affects Lazy Asses when they're about to say 'I do'. Professor Ben Fletcher, Head of Psychology at the University of Hertfordshire, shares his wealth of knowledge into the cogs of the male brain. 'It's not so much that men are lazy, it's more the fact that weddings are notoriously a female thing. Usually brides, mothers and mothers-in-law get involved and plan the day together. Traditionally women are brought up to dream about their wedding day, men aren't. Therefore the wedding day has more significance to women for a longer period of time. Also, many of the details like the flowers and clothing are feminine in orientation. It's not that men don't value the wedding day as much, it's just more a female thing.'

Maybe us brides are just too hard on them? Christine, from Relate: 'For many men, weddings are a time when they start to ask themselves serious questions: is she the right one for me? Does she really represent who I am, who I want to be? Do my mates like her? They also start looking inwardly about their own family, and whether they'll like his new wife.'

So on the whole, weddings are more for ladies than the men-folk. But as long as you know from the outset that you're not going to see him do a celebratory lap of the living-room when you announce you've finally found napkins the same shade as the chief bridesmaid's pants, you won't be disappointed. And you won't spend hours waiting for him to do things; you'll just do them yourself or delegate it to a female member of the bridal party.

The thing that I struggled with was: surely the day is about both of you? Why should he expect to get away with doing nothing, and then turn up on the big day and graciously take all the slaps on the back for a job well done?

Five top tips for motivating Lazy Ass

- Remind him, it's an excuse to get drunk three times: stag do, wedding day and honeymoon. If he's lucky, at some point the opportunity of a lap dance might arise. Be that on the stag do, or during the wedding reception by one of the bridesmaids, a bladdered bride or mucky Aunt Maud!
- Weddings are an opportunity for two holidays: stag do and the honeymoon. The honeymoon being the prime chance to chat with women in bikinis.
- It's a chance to look polished and dapper in front of female friends/family members that he's always fancied – the wedding is the perfect excuse to kiss them all.
- Some crusty old goats might view it as morally wrong, but stuff them. Use the power of 'bedroom services' to entice him to do things on your list.
- Buy him a football and let him kick it in the house.

A lesson in all-things-wedding

So, if Lazy Ass doesn't know that much about weddings, then it's up to us brides, as wedding connoisseurs, to educate him. While ladies have a plethora of magazines, television programmes, websites and books dedicated to what women want for their wedding, Lazy Ass might have to dig around.

On first look, it seems there's no *Groom's Monthly* or *Grooming for Grooms*; filled with glossy pages of chaps lounging around sipping Tetley from champagne flutes, while discussing the latest in cravats. But have a sniff around and there is stuff out there to help. Clothing store Moss Bros publishes a magazine called *The Guide – Everything You Need To Know About Formal Style* which is worth a flick through. It offers Lazy Asses down-to-earth advice on what they need to do and when, and also some style tips. For those bone-idle guys who really don't have a clue, then try www.groomservice.co.uk – an online wedding godfather for males who need help hiring their suits, writing their speech or just need a shoulder to cry on.

Most wedding websites have sections for Lazy Ass and even message boards where soon-to-be-wed males can hide out and bitch about their brides. Have a quick nosey and there are actually men in the chatrooms, discussing everything from fantasy football, to who is going to be the next signing at Arsenal, plus some cheeky rascals flogging their cars.

Inspire Them

We've scoured the world and the web and squeezed a handful of wedding boffins dry to get some top tips to help you inspire even the most gormless of grooms.

Groom's To Do List		Tick
1 year to go	*Tell everyone*	❏
8 months	*Decide on style of wedding,*	❏
	when and where	❏
7 months	*Book venue and pay deposit*	❏
6 months	*Choose your best man and ushers*	❏
	Plan your honeymoon	❏
5 months	*Decide what to wear*	❏
	Work on wedding guest list	❏
4 months	*Discuss stag night with best man*	❏
	Book photographer	❏
	and order wedding cake	❏
3 months	*Order stationery*	❏
	Pick suit and order wedding outfits	❏
2 months	*Send out invites*	❏
	Final arrangements	❏
1 month	*Ensure honeymoon and*	❏
	flights are booked	❏
2 weeks	*Re-check honeymoon details*	❏
	Arrange currency	❏
1 week	*Enjoy stag do!*	❏
	Collect wedding outfit	❏
	Write speech	❏

'Give the groom a to-do list. But be realistic, don't expect him to have an opinion on everything. Give him things he will want to do, and will actually do. How about choosing the bridal cars, the wine, or the presents for the best man, ushers and fathers? Understand that he is interested, but the most obvious sign of excitement you're likely to get is a yes, no, or a lift of an eyebrow. They're never going to be as excited about it as you.'

Wedding guru Rebecca Hulme-Edwardson

'You can get married wherever you like now, so this should inspire more men to think about what they want. Getting married under the sea or on top of a mountain gives grooms more scope to get involved and have their say.'

Mind-man and psychologist, Professor Ben Fletcher

Left, from *The Guide – Everything You Wanted To Know About Formal Style* (Moss Bros). Reproduced with kind permission.

Motivational mantras

Nature gave man two ends – one to think with and one to sit on. A man's success depends on which end he uses most; a case of heads you win, tails you lose.

George R. Kirkpatrick

A day merely survived is no cause for celebration.

Og Mandino

A great pleasure in life is doing what people say you cannot do.

Walter Bagehot

Every mother generally hopes that her daughter will snag a better husband than she managed to do... but she's certain that her boy will never get as great a wife as his father did.

Anon

Bridal behaviour

wedding Mag

BE A BLUSHING BRIDEZILLA!

I LOVE BEING MARRIED.

IT'S SO GREAT TO FIND THAT

ONE SPECIAL PERSON YOU WANT

TO ANNOY FOR THE REST OF

YOUR LIFE.

Rita Rudner

The last chapter was about bloke-bashing; now it's time to turn the tables and laugh at ludicrous and inappropriate bridal behaviour. We've all heard of this Bridezilla creature and, as a bride-to-be, you'll begin to understand her that little bit better.

We all experience the odd bad bout of wedding mania. No matter how organised or focussed you are, there will be something along the way that will send you spinning, get under your skin and make you want to blow. In short, get right on your nerves. That could be a nosey future mother-in-law, bone-idle bridesmaid, wayward supplier or just Lazy Ass getting in your way. Whatever it is will seem colossal and threaten to jeopardise your future happiness. But, if you stop and think for a minute, you'll know deep down you're blowing things way out of proportion, but it won't make any difference.

Bridezilla's Wedding Venue Criteria

- Can I flounce around the place?
- Is there a room for civil ceremony that doesn't look like a conference venue?
- Will the champagne be flowing constantly?
- Is the food and drink excellent? I don't want boiled chicken and hard veg.
- Is there enough room for everyone to stay?
- Does the residents' bar stay open past 3am?
- Is the dance floor big enough to cope with 100 20/30-somethings making a show of themselves dancing to The Stone Roses?

We did a survey of wives and brides and asked them:
Why do women get totally obsessed with weddings?

Brides on being Bridezilla:

*'I knew I'd be excited about planning the wedding, but
never thought I'd turn into the bitch from hell. It just
happened – I overdosed on wedding magazines wedding
fairs and got annoyed with people asking me about the
date, so took it out on Lazy Ass. He'd done nothing to
help, so I enjoyed wedding-bashing him. I now know
why I got all uptight; I'm rubbish at making decisions
and totally disorganised.'*

Bridezilla

*'There are so many people telling you what you "should
have" for your day, it's hard not to get a bit freaked out.
Celebrity weddings are plastered all over the media and
the pressure to make your day better or different from
your friends is immense. It's just that feeling that the
more money you spend, the better it'll be!'*

Judith

*'Women just want everything to be perfect, but the
way for that to happen is to just relax – which isn't
always easy.'*

Lynn

'The obsession just comes over you. I got obsessed more the week before making sure everything was just right and in order. While I was sorting everything out, my other half was sat on his backside watching Man U!'

Emma

'The most stressful thing for me is the fact that our wedding will be the first time my divorced parents have met, let alone spoken, for about ten years. Everyone at work has decided we'd better play Kaiser Chiefs' "I Predict a Riot" as I walk down the aisle.'

Heather

'When a woman is planning her wedding and something goes wrong it's like watching an animal escaping from a predator. There's loads of screeching, arm waving and feet stamping – all that noise over something as stupid as the colour of a blooming balloon.'

Lazy Ass

If the groom's mother throws an old shoe over (not at!) the new bride as they leave the ceremony location, the bride and her mother-in-law will be friends forever!

Anon

Bridal stress

In addition to the moody swings that organising a wedding can induce, there can also be night traumas to contend with. One minute you're sleeping soundly, the next you're wide awake troubled with irrelevant thoughts. My sleep-stoppers seem ridiculous now, but at the time, they were serious issues:

- At 5ft 2¹/₂ inches, I was never going to be that beautiful 5ft 9 inches bride smiling up from the front cover of my favourite wedding magazine. The one, that in my mind, I was going to turn into on the morning of my big day. I had to admit that I could do almost everything else I wanted for my wedding day, but there was no way I could muster another seven inches. Not even in heels. I eventually shed the rage by punching the model bride on the cover very hard in the face.
- Bouts of OCD brought on by wedding fairs, the Aladdin's cave of weddings. These events are nothing but overcrowded, overheated hotel rooms filled to the brim with paraphernalia of 'essential' tat for your wedding. So essential I didn't even know the stuff existed before entering the room, and I still didn't really have a clue as to what they were when I left, with an invoice for 150 of 'something' in my back pocket. Even after spending five Saturdays on the bounce traipsing round the

blasted things, I still couldn't help but get butterflies whenever I saw another one advertised in the local paper. What kept me awake? I thought I'd miss an essential product if I didn't go.

- It's hard to believe it now but the glitzy ring on my left hand, the one I tap-danced over, actually caused me grief. It felt like it was a sign to the world that I was now a responsible, lady-like adult-turned event planner, capable of pulling everything off while keeping a cool head. When I knew, and all around knew that I wasn't – and I'm still not!

It's no wonder Julia Roberts does a runner so many times in that cheesy old classic *Runaway Bride*, or Canadian bride-to-be Jennifer Wilbanks faked her own kidnap and scarpered shortly before her own big day. What if you're not perfect bride material? We're not all born with the DNA to make us turn into Wonder Bride, no matter how hard our mother might scrub. The Reverend Laurie Sue Brockway is every bride's Fairy Godmother. The popular New York-based non-denominational wedding officiant, is widely recognised as a bridal stress expert devoted to helping brides-to-be tap into their inner power and poise. In her book, *Wedding Goddess: A Divine Guide to Transforming Wedding Stress into Wedding Bliss*, she serves up endless slices of 'calm down pie' to brides on the edge.

Fresh from the page, here are her five top tips:

1. It's supposed to be the happiest time of your life – and you want it to be – yet planning a wedding is like working a second job. You have to find the time to tend to a multitude of details as part of an already busy schedule while managing vendors, family anxieties and demands, your groom, your emotions and an array of tricky wedding dynamics.

   Wedding Goddess Antidote: A bride has to include stress management, self-nurturing and time to chill out as an integral part of her wedding planning process. When you feel the stress building, take time out, go for a walk, slip into a movie, get a massage, go for a manicure, write in a journal, do something un-wedding. You have to love, honour and cherish yourself if you want to be loved, honoured and cherished by someone else!

2. No matter who you are or what age... everyone has something to say about your wedding. You may be showered with congratulations and gifts, but you are simultaneously bombarded with unsolicited advice and negative vibes from well-meaning friends and relatives who are too lost in their own experience to realise they are imposing on you. People tend to see your wedding as a chance to fulfil their own needs. Family dynamics erupt in

every which direction because, as the clan prepares to gather, they begin to act out, and the feelings once hidden and kept in reserve may bubble to the surface.

Wedding Goddess Antidote: A bride has to clarify the wedding she truly wants, try to stay centred and set clear boundaries that no one can penetrate with words or attitudes. If all else fails, consider this: the reality is that weddings tend to be for other people, but marriage is for you two. Focus on what your marriage will mean to you.

3. Getting married can stir up a lot of emotions. The process itself sets forth a period of growth and change that can be very confusing and nerve-wracking. This doesn't mean you shouldn't marry, it just means inner work is called for along with all the outer preparations.

Wedding Goddess Antidote: A bride can embrace the awareness that she is embarking on a journey of evolution from one part of life to another, and honour and address the emotions and fears that arise. Trust they are natural and pay attention to any issues that might require support or counselling. It is important to stay on top of your emotions and be honest with yourself during this time. Don't sweep things under the rug.

4. Wedding planning can be a crisis. There is so much focus on the external experience that a bride can become mired in details and demands and lose track of herself and the reason she is getting married in the first place. When she feels that planning the wedding of her dreams means going to battle – with parents, family, friends, groom, and almost anyone involved – she becomes hostile and reactive. What began as a joyful experience turns into a fight... a fight for having the perfect wedding. It is exhausting and can turn even sweet-tempered people can turn mean and cranky.

Wedding Goddess Antidote: Remember that the true meaning of marriage is to bring two people together in sacred union – the party is meant to be a celebration, not something that will kill your spirit in the planning.

5. Your happiness in life DOES NOT hinge on your wedding alone (it really doesn't... so lighten up!). Some brides believe that they must have a perfect wedding in order to have a perfect marriage and a perfect life. They give the wedding day too much power. They begin to treat the wedding itself as something to be worshipped and served.

Wedding Goddess Antidote: Step back and realise the most important part of the day is not the day itself... but that you walked down that aisle and into the arms of the person you love... the one you look forward to building your life with.

Reproduced with kind permission.

Rev. Laurie Sue Brockway's de-stressing tips:

Stay close to your groom: You will cut your stress in half if you two remain a united team. You won't see eye to eye on all things... but you must stand together and back each other up when it comes to making decisions. When well-meaning-but-meddling relatives try to sway you, stay strong and hold on tight to one another!

Savour the small stuff: From the day you become engaged, to the moment you say, 'I do' make every moment count. Savour even the little things you do to make your wedding special. Keep the focus that the Big Day is a sacred day. It is not just a party that needs planning... it is a marriage that you are preparing for. All these little things along the way are helping you prepare.

Manage your time on your wedding day. Nothing is more flustering to a bride than running late on your wedding day. Create a timeline that includes everything from your morning coffee, to leaving for the ceremony, and stick as close to it as possible. Take control of time on your wedding day so that it does not add stress to the natural butterflies in the tummy.

Stay present: Don't risk missing it all, or remembering it as a blur, because you were too busy agonizing over the details and the drama. Trust that your wedding will unfold as it is meant to be and will be perfect for you. If you can stay present – rather than worrying or dazing out – you can look one another in the eyes at the wedding altar and remember the power of that moment!

Visit www.weddinggoddess.com for more de-stress Bridezilla tips.

The bridal flaps

Christine Northam, from Relate, dishes out some reassuring advice for brides at the end of their tether and grooms heading out to the pub for some shelter from the abuse. 'Marriage is about what you represent and your status. You're making a public statement in front of the people you care about. In many ways you're putting yourself on the line and insecurities under the surface can very easily bubble to the top. So you're bound to get hot under the collar.' Soothing words from an expert. 'During the build-up to the wedding, women enjoy getting carried away with the pretty side of the day, the location, the dress – it's really a feminine thing. At the back of their minds there is a voice saying 'will the day be everything I dreamt of and will I really get what I want?' It is a stressful time. Then there's the added stress of arguing with the other half. Most women don't let men get involved, but then moan when they don't do anything. Start as you mean to go on, practise working together collaboratively on the wedding and it will continue into married life.'

Wedding planner Rebecca Hulme-Edwardson knows only too well what it's like when the wedding enthusiasm makes the cork pop off. 'Obviously brides are going to get excited about their big day. But sometimes it doesn't stop there. I've had to fire-fight a few bride-and-sister battles over the years. One particular wedding the sister wouldn't let the bride have any say in the arrangements. Every time the bride gave a suggestion, her sister would laugh at it and then suggest something else. In the end the bride burst into tears and I had to step in.'

Advice for Lazy Ass: Coping with the bridal flaps

'I find giving her a glass of wine and the remote control often helps. Or the phone so she can call her mother.'

Lazy Ass

'Newly-engaged men would do well to heed the advice my father-in-law gave to me when I first got engaged: "Keep your head down and let the women folk take care of everything".'

Anton from the rugby club

'Look interested and pick the worst of everything that you know she won't like. She won't ask again and you'll have an easy life.'

Marsy

Professor Ben Fletcher offers some sound advice to grooms on how to understand that new psychotic partner. 'Weddings for most women are a symbolic and important event. They enjoy the whole planning process and ensuring everything, down to the smallest detail, is spot on. It's important to them and men should respect that. Try and put yourself in their shoes, and understand when they get slightly irate or upset about something. Don't just disappear out the door if they get emotional about something – offer your support. In fact if both the bride and groom think about it from the other person's point of view – it will make for a good wedding and also a good marriage.'

General advice for Lazy Ass:

'Give her a half hour a night to just go on about wedding issues that trouble her. Just let her blow off steam, and complain. Listen. Know she's been planning for this day all her life. Support her. Say "yes" a lot.'

Rev. Laurie Sue Brockway

'If you're abroad when popping the question, then go the whole hog and get married while you're away. Enjoy the big party when you get back. Alternatively make the big decisions quickly and then let her enjoy doing all the donkey work! Make a decision and then get it all over and done with.'

Lazy Ass

'Learn how to throw a deaf ear.'

Marsy

'Don't look at the telly when she talks to you and tell her she's right when she's not!'

John

'As a bloke watching your future wife plan your wedding, you should realise that for the most part you are wrong and she is right and that she will always get what she wants in the end. Apply that logic to the rest of your married life and remember it is much easier to swim with the current.'

Wolfy

'Alternatively you could just ignore her when she starts talking and go to the pub. Not too good if you want a quiet life!'

Wolfy again!

'Weddings are all about pleasing two very special people: the bride and her mother.'

Anon

Bridesmaids beware

It is not just Lazy Ass that will feel the bridal bristle; brides-maids are also in the direct firing line of the dragonbreath. From chatting with other brides, it seems bridesmaids tend to feel it most if they show any dislike of the dress that the bride has picked out. Bernie, from London, got a kick when she wrinkled her nose up at the salmon-coloured gown that her mate Mandy had chosen. 'For a start, the dress was hideous. Big puffy sleeves and a large bow perched right where my backside would be. It looked like something out of an '80s teen movie,' recalls Bernie. 'It didn't stop there though – the colour was just awful – it was skin-colour and made me look naked. When I first saw the dress I tried to hide my horror, but didn't actually do it that well. I just refused to wear it; Mandy had a massive moody, kicked me really hard in the middle of the shop and ran off. In the end, none of the other bridesmaids liked it. We found a burnt-orange colour that was still disgusting, but looked a little bit better. She never apologised for kicking me, the cheeky brat.'

A bride from Melbourne, who wishes to remain nameless, admitted to being so cheesed off with her bridesmaids for not liking the dresses she'd had made for them, that she sacked them from their positions. She replaced her sister and best friend, with a girl from work (whom she'd only known for three weeks) and the groom's cousin, whom she didn't know very well. 'Whenever we talk about the wedding, I cringe. I know I totally overreacted and shouldn't have stopped them from being my bridesmaids. At the time, I felt like they just wanted to spoil my day and were jealous because neither of them were married. My mother has never forgiven me.'

We have all heard of brides that go diet-crazy just to look matchstick-thin on their big day. Sometimes bridesmaids forgo a little bit too much food so they can look lovely. But brides across the world don't seem to appreciate the weight loss. Beth from New Jersey, Carla from London, Tara from Rotherham, Sandra from Vancouver, and Nancie from Dublin, all demoted their bridesmaids to mere wedding guests after they lost so much weight. 'It sounds so fickle now, but for me it was about wanting to be the prettiest and thinnest person at my wedding,' explains Tara, shaking her head. 'Both of my bridesmaids were heavier than I was, and I didn't think for a minute one of them would lose a lot of weight. My friend, Kim, went on a mad exercise and health kick eight months before the wedding. She dropped from around 12 stones to 9 stones and looked fantastic. I couldn't handle her new look and didn't want her on my wedding photographs, so I told her I'd decided to just have my niece as a bridesmaid because of lack of money, even though she'd already been for a dress fitting.'

If you feel yourself getting a little hot-under-the-collar with your special ladies, take a deep breath, call up your best fake smile and excuse yourself from the situation. It might be your wedding day but that doesn't give you the right to dress your friends up like muppets to make you look better. Ask your bridesmaids what they'd like to wear, go shopping together and try lots of outfits on until you find something that you both like. Team your outfit shopping with lunch and a few cheeky cocktails and you're guaranteed success.

The name game

A survey by *You and Your Wedding* magazine in 2006 asked readers: Will you be changing your name? A whopping 87.43 percent said 'yes' and a mere 12.57 percent said 'no'. It seems that the feminists among us are losing the battle in campaigning to keep your maiden name once you're married. The consensus is no one really cares any more and it's just more hassle than it's worth.

Rebecca Hulme-Edwardson obviously is in the minority and can offer brides first-hand advice. 'I kept my name because I'm the last one in the family to get married and we're all girls. Besides it's who I am and who I was born. With hindsight, having a double-barrelled name is a nightmare and I don't think I would do it again. People get it wrong and your name is so long. Then, what if you have children? Some brides keep their maiden name for work purposes and then change it in their personal life. All the couples I've done weddings for have changed their name, it really isn't a big deal any more.'

'I've always been adamant that I'm not changing my name and that isn't going to change. No matter how many of the my mates raise their eyebrows, snigger into their G&Ts or write birthday cards to the future Mrs Reed, I'm not biting.'

Bridezilla

'No matter what, women can't win; if you change your name you become your mother-in-law and if you keep your surname – become your mother... I'm not sure which is worse!'

Joanna

'I have changed my name, but I kept my maiden name and this is now my middle name.'

Emma

'Changing my name represented a new beginning as a married woman. I liked the idea of being one family, with one name and I also like tradition. I think some women read too much into changing their name.'

Clare

'*I might leave it as it is or have it double-barrelled, even though the other half isn't too chuffed about it. But, my get-out clause is that my fiancé says he won't wear a ring when we're married as he doesn't like jewellery.*'

Heather

'*I have changed my name on everything apart from at work because nobody could spell it and it drove me nuts having to repeat myself all the time.*'

Mazza

As with everything else attached to your wedding, the name game is prime target for the world to offer its opinions. But it's your name, so do as you please.

Your options (and their problems):

1. Become a Mrs and take his surname – become Mrs Reed (like his mother!).
2. Stay Miss Dugdale (makes you sound very young or like an 80-year-old spinster).
3. Ms Reed (some say Ms makes people think you're a lesbian or hard-nosed woman with a point to prove).
4. Mrs/Ms Dugdale-Reed or Ms Dugdale Reed (granted, your pretentiousness factor does rise if your surname's double-barrelled, but the more people say it, the more it just becomes your name!).

If you choose the double-barrelled option, with or without the hyphen, you will need to apply to change your name by deed poll which can be done before or after the wedding. For more details, contact the UK Deed Poll Service www.ukdps.co.uk

Wedding costumes

IT BEGINS WITH A PRINCE
KISSING AN ANGEL. IT ENDS
WITH A BALD-HEADED MAN
LOOKING ACROSS THE TABLE
AT A FAT WOMAN.

Anon

Ahhh! The dress, every little girl's dream frock. Whoever you are, however tall, however wide your waistline or whatever the circumference of your calves, you know you're guaranteed to look absolutely cracking when you find the dress.

But, what is the secret to getting the perfect one for you? Do you need the budget the size of Paris Hilton's bank balance to find the dress? Which style will suit you best? If you're experienced in the bedroom, does that mean you can't wear white? Does ivory look mucky? And what would Lazy Ass look good in?

Stress no more ladies, we've trekked the highlands and the lowlands and stolen all the secrets of how to get you so scrubbed-up you'll sparkle.

A Good Old Fashioned Wedding Dress Poem

Married in White, you have chosen right,
Married in Grey, you will go far away,
Married in Black, you will wish yourself back,
Married in Red, you will wish yourself dead,
Married in Green, ashamed to be seen,
Married in Blue, you will always be true,
Married in Pearl, you will live in a whirl,
Married in Yellow, ashamed of your fellow,
Married in Brown, you will live in the town,
Married in Pink, your spirit will sink.

The dress

From the grand gowns that swing freely on the 18-carat gold racks in the stores of Vera Wang, Caroline Castigliano and Phillipa Lepley, to Designers at Debenhams. Take a deep breath and smile, because right now the dress is out there and all you've got to do is enjoy the hunt to find it.

According to research by Mintel, the average cost of a wedding dress has rocketed 32 per cent since the start of the millennium to an average price tag of more than £800. That's some serious spend on a dress that you normally only wear once.

Before you hit those bridal shops you've been licking the windows of, take a look at the top 10 things to think about:

- The venue and style of your wedding can offer clues to the kind of dress that is right for the day.
- Flick through wedding magazines and collate a pile of pictures/images of dresses and styles you like. Take these along to the appointment with the dressmaker, boutique, or store.
- Most bridal boutiques and stores ask you to make an appointment so they can go through the styles and ranges of dresses on offer.
- Wear suitable (clean!) underwear, a bra that fits well and underwear that is white or neutral colours.

- Don't forget to take a pair of heels.
- Take along someone whose opinion you trust: your mum, sister, best mate. Someone who isn't going to take the mickey and encourage you to buy a meringue. Someone who has your best interest at heart and will tell you the truth.
- It's a process of elimination – be prepared to try on many different styles, including some that you wouldn't normally have chosen. Dresses that you don't like on the hanger often come to life when you try them on.
- Let yourself be guided by your instinct and the expert advice at hand. Remember guests will spend most of the ceremony looking at your back(side).
- Consider the fabric – go for floaty, soft material if you want a figure-hugging dress and heavier fabric if you want to hide lumps and bumps.
- Each time you try something on, look at the dress and decide why you like it/don't like it: is it the neckline, the fullness of skirt or the fabric?

Kate Webster owns bridal store Lace, which she opened after her own nightmare of trying to find that fantastic frock. 'As much as it's important to look through magazines and get an idea of what it is you want, it's more important to keep an open mind. You've got to realise that you might end up walking down the aisle in something you might never have imagined. Listen to the consultants in the shop and what your instincts are telling you.'

Kate's expert wedding dress advice:

- The bigger the skirt, the smaller your waist will look.
- Leave your fashion sense at the shop door and open your mind. You'll be surprised what you might end up buying.
- Expect to pay 50 percent deposit when you order the dress. Don't pay the remaining balance until you have tried the dress on.
- Beware of scripted sales consultants who don't give you their honest opinion of what you really look like in that expensive dress.
- Ask the consultant if any alternations will be needed once the gown has been delivered. Most stores charge additional alteration fees for minor adjustments.
- Expect to sign some kind of disclaimer form. Read this carefully and check all the details are correct.

If fighting over your chosen gown with all the other brides-to-be out there doesn't sound like fun, then why not do what loads of other brides are doing and buy your dress online? Check out sites like:

www.ebay.com
www.almostnewweddingdresses.co.uk
www.thedressmarket.com
www.netbrides.com and
www.elegancebridalstudio.co.uk

UK brides can also check www.oxfam.org.uk for stores that have bridal departments. You can get both second-hand and new dresses online and save yourself a fortune. Also check out the message boards of wedding sites where brides are often selling their wedding wear. Just make sure the site you're buying from is reputable.

Something different

Not every bride-to-be wants to float down the aisle in a pretty white or ivory flowing gown. Some women aspire to something a little bit different and want to create a massive 'wow factor'. You've only got to look in the direction of the celeb world for some inspiration. Andrea Catherwood, the British newsreader, made headlines when she walked down the aisle wearing an eye-catching wedding dress with a bare midriff, which revealed her pierced belly button. Good old Katie Price, aka Jordan, wore a two-metre wide, Barbie-pink gown with a corset made from thousands of pink Swarovski crystals and a six-metre-long train. To top the outfit off, she sported a pink crown more than a foot high. Katie arrived at Highclere Castle, Berkshire, in a glass Cinderella-style carriage that featured baby pink satin seats and a pink fur carpet. Her enormous dress didn't actually fit into the carriage, so she wore a tiny sequinned tutu, and then changed into the dress. For something more off-the-wall, follow in the footsteps of Angelina Jolie. When she married Jonny Lee Miller, she wore black leather trousers and a white shirt. On the back of her shirt, in her own blood, she wrote her husband's name. If that's a bit too Count Dracula, then why not opt for a revealing bikini, Pammy Anderson-style? Too hard to make the decision? Then why not have more than one frock, Liz Hurley-style? For her wedding in England, Liz wore a white dress designed by Donatella Versace, and for her ceremony in India she went all-out in a wedding sari.

Want the perfect princess wedding? Then Walt Disney has unveiled a range of 34 bridal dresses inspired by films like *Sleeping Beauty* and *Beauty and the Beast* that cost between £755 and £1,500. Why not go the whole hog and choose a full-on Disney-themed wedding with rides in a Cinderella carriage and appearances by Mickey and Minnie Mouse dressed-up to the nines?

An eco-friendly frock

If you're feeling green and want to do your bit for the environment on your big day, then how about an eco-friendly frock? What most brides don't think about when ordering their dress is where it comes from and who made it. Pity really, because all too often wedding dresses are made in sweatshops somewhere in the Far East, where there are huge problems with exploitation and dreadful working conditions. Then, add in the air miles and CO_2 emissions because the dress has to be carted back to where the bride lives, and you begin to realise that weddings actually aren't very good for the environment. But you can do your bit. When choosing your gown try and avoid polyester because it's made from petrochemicals, meaning it's non-biodegradable and involves an awful lot of water and energy to make. Surprisingly silk is also a no-no, because silk worms are often boiled alive or electrocuted in order to extract silk from its cocoon – nice!

Finding a good-for-the-environment gown isn't as hard as you probably think. There are loads of shops and websites that do them.

Try:
www.wholly-jo.co.uk
www.organicweddings.com
www.weddingwardrobe.co.uk and
www.threadheadcreations.com

You can make your whole wedding green if you wish, simply by working out your carbon emissions and buying credits to offset them. There are loads of organisations set-up to help with this, including www.carbonplanet.com and www.thecarbonneutralcompany.co.uk

What's the veil all about?

Traditionally, the bride wore a veil as a form of modesty. It kept her face hidden from the groom as she walked down the aisle. The idea was to pull back the veil so that the groom could see his future wife's face.

The lifting of the veil at the end of the ceremony symbolises male dominance. If the bride takes the initiative in lifting it, thereby presenting herself to him, she is showing more independence.

Something old...

Something old – symbolises the continuity and stability of marriage. As the bride leaves her single life to join her new husband, it is also seen as a promise to keep her old friends and remember her family.

Something new – symbolises a new beginning, the making of new friends, of new fortune and adventure.

Something borrowed – symbolises close relations' or friends' love and support. A bride will borrow an item from a happily married woman to bring her good luck in her married life.

Something blue – in biblical times, blue was worn to represent purity, love and fidelity.

Shoes

Bridal footwear has moved on from the days when there were just two styles to choose from: safe satin court shoes or cheap-looking white stilettos. These days most designers and high street stores offer a bridal collection with shoes that can be worn again. At the top end of the shoe rack sits the delights of Emma Hope and Jimmy Choo, and at the other end Ravel, Next, Dolcis and Faith.

Wedding Planner Rebecca Hulme-Edwardson shares her two-penneth: 'Brides are tending to steer away from "bridal shoes". They've realised there is no point in spending £200 on a pair of cream satin court shoes that they're never going to wear again. Some things to consider: watch the height of your heel – you don't want to be taller than the groom. A couple of inches is fine – something you're not going to break your ankle on if you fall off them!'

As with other areas of weddings, nightmare stories creep out of the woodwork. Hairdresser Michael Peckett has a wealth of hilarious bridal stories. 'We can all learn something from the bride who bought a fantastic pair of shoes that finished her outfit off perfectly,' laughs Michael. 'Being particularly organised, she sanded the bottom of her shoes to stop them for slipping. On the morning of her wedding she took the shoes out of the box, but when she went to put them on she realised she had two left shoes! As usual, mum saved the day by nipping down the high street to buy another pair.'

Cut out the stress and wear the shoes around the house to make sure you can walk in them, and you're not going to do a Naomi Campbell down the aisle.

Turkish shoe-signing tradition

Try a who-will-marry-next tradition that Turkish brides have been practising for generations. Before you start down the aisle, have any female friends or relatives who've yet to marry sign the sole of your bridal shoe. After you've danced the night away, legend has it that the person whose name has faded the most will be the next to marry.

Bloke costumes

Now, let's shift our gaze to the gentleman of the day, Lazy Ass. The groom's outfit isn't as hard to find as the bride's, but it can still take some time to decide in just what outfit they want to trot down the aisle.

Whether they choose to go for the traditional morning suit from a high street store like Moss Bros or a more hip, tailored look from the likes of Armani or Paul Smith, it's all about two things: colour and style.

Kate Hipkins from Pronuptia has been offering advice to soon-to-be-grooms for over 14 years. 'These days there are no hard and fast rules about what men wear at weddings.

We live in a casual society and not as many people wear suits to work, so when you do wear a wedding suit, it can feel different. It's important to think about what you want to wear on your big day, and try on a variety of styles. Give yourself some time to get used to wearing the tie and the waistcoat. Also think about the colours; it looks great if a groom and male attendant co-ordinate well with the rest of the wedding.'

Kate's top five things for grooms to think about:

1. Style – what's the style of the wedding: traditional or informal?

   STYLE OF COAT:
   Tails – traditional wedding
   Prince Edward – three quarter length jacket (suits informal wedding)
   Short – similar to regular suit jacket (suits informal wedding)

2. Colour – it's always good to co-ordinate with the wedding colours. But what tones and shades suit you? There are no strict rules about what people should wear, but most grooms wear a different tie and waistcoat to ushers and the best man.

3. When you go to try on suits, it's recommended to take someone with you – either the bride, best man or an usher. But taking too many people along to the appointment can mean that what the groom really wants is lost in the drone of other people's opinions.

4. It's not just the suit you need to think about. The tie and waistcoat are also important. Remember, after the formal part of the day is over, the chances are you'll whip the jacket off and parade around in your shirt and waistcoat.

As with the ladies' outfits, it's really important to go for fittings and also try the suits on when you collect them. That way you'll avoid the nightmare of a best man with a beer gut trying to squeeze into a waistcoat that was meant for the scrawny ginger usher. Stevie from Manchester knows all about this with his white suit saga. 'Ordering the suits wasn't the problem. It was when we came to collect them that the nightmare began. They weren't ready for collection until two days before the wedding, instead of the five as promised. Then once I'd collected them I had to drive around the neighbourhood dropping them off. First my dad rang – his waistcoat was the wrong size. Then I got a call from my sister – one of my nephews' jacket was the wrong size, one waistcoat was a different style and a cravat was missing. Then the phone rang again and it was two of the ushers moaning that their waistcoats were the wrong size. The shop eventually replaced the wrong items, except my nephew's jacket. But the new items weren't delivered until the morning of the wedding. Then during the wedding breakfast, I took my jacket off and noticed my shirt had a rip on the shoulder. Luckily I'd taken a spare shirt because I knew I'd spill something down me during the night. After weeks of complaining the store finally offered us £250 compensation. It didn't affect the wedding, but it was grief I could have done without.'

Ladies beware: some smart-ass grooms like to have a little joke between themselves and the wedding guests. Nick, a thirty-something Brit who now lives in Spain, was one of these sneaky gentlemen. During his wedding service he and the bride had to kneel down. Unbeknown to the bride – and just for a laugh – Nick had sellotaped the words 'Help' and 'Me' to the underneath of his shoes. When the guests saw it, the church erupted, making the bride extremely paranoid!

Anti-wedding attire

On an average day, most blokes flop out of bed, grab a pair of crusty boxers, pull on a pair of grubby trousers and a sweaty shirt and roll out the door. For some scummy devils this routine doesn't change on their wedding day. Jed, from Byron Bay, Australia, left shopping for his wedding outfit until the morning of the big day. Unable to find a pair of trousers to fit him because he's 6ft 6inches, he rolled up to the church in a pink shirt and tie, grey suit jacket, black socks and shiny lace-up shoes, and a pair of orange and lime green boarding shorts. The bride thought it was hilarious.

Mark, from Dublin, was almost as bad. On the morning of the wedding he lazed around the place having a fag and a breakfast of Doritos and Guinness. When the time arrived for him to get ready, he switched on the iron and filled it up with what he thought was water from the glass on the ironing board. It was only when the iron started to fizz and the liquid bubbled out of it, that Mark realised the liquid was actually lemonade. His new navy blue Ozwald Boateng shirt was streaked with sticky iron marks and smelt of burnt sugar. Undeterred, he wore the shirt anyway and kept his suit jacket on until he thought the bride and his mother had drunk enough that they wouldn't notice.

Then there was the groom, the best man and two ushers who turned up at the church dressed in their Welsh rugby shirts, jeans and mucky trainers. It wasn't intentional – they'd all been out for a quiet drink the evening before, but got a bit too boisterous, and ended up breaking into their old junior school (to see if their names were still written in the toilets!). The idiots were caught red-handed and spent the night in the local police cells. They had to make the decision to go home and get changed or get to the church on time. They arrived panting and red-faced with six minutes to spare.

If Lazy Ass doesn't fancy the thought of being trussed-up in a shirt and tie on his big day, be fair; you have to give the bloke a break and try to find a compromise. When you ask him what he wants to wear, before you put your head in your hands with despair, actually listen to what he has to say.

We asked a few soon-to-be-wed blokes what they would really like to wear to their wedding.

'My rugby socks, a bobble hat, a glitzy thong and my mum's flowery nightgown.'

Lazy Ass

'A superhero outfit; I'd be Spiderman and the wife could be Lara Croft.'

Sam

'A Leicester City shirt and my football slippers.'

Anton

'I've always wanted to be a boxer – so I'd love to wear long red shiny shorts and a big cape with a hood. The bride would wear a bikini and parade round the place with the scorecards.'

John

Hearing what men really want to wear might bring on a hot flush; but remember... deep breaths plus a bottle of vodka, and you're guaranteed to come to a compromise.

Wedding essentials

THE MOST DANGEROUS
FOOD A MAN CAN EAT IS
WEDDING CAKE!

Anon

It's boring but essential: let's talk insurance. Your first reaction might be, 'You're having a laugh – why do I need insurance?' But, if you shut up for a minute and think logically about it, there are good reasons for taking out some cover. Wedding insurance expert Andy Newman explains: 'The average wedding costs around £20,000. If you spent that amount of money on a deposit on a house or bought a new car, you'd get insurance, so why not for your wedding?' Couples tying the knot in 2006 spent a staggering £4.4billion on their weddings – and yet four-out-of-five of them didn't take out insurance to protect themselves against things going wrong. As we've discovered, not everything always goes to plan on the big day, so insurance would give you that extra peace of mind. You can get wedding insurance from as little as £54, which will give you £7,500 worth of cover. Not a lot when you're spending so much on that frock.

Most Common Wedding Insurance Claims:

- Loss of deposit through failure of supplier – wedding venue goes bust or supplier disappears into the night with your cash.
- Damage to wedding attire, e.g. fag burn on wedding dress, red wine on best man's suit, vomit in mother-in-law's hat.
- Theft from wedding venue, e.g. some cheeky rascal robs your new crystal cake stand.
- Illness of key members of wedding party, e.g. Granny Trudy breaks her leg doing a drunken rendition of the can-can.
- Cancellation of wedding due to relocation, or members of wedding party called up for jury service.
- Restaging of wedding photographs due to damage to film or equipment.

Things you can't claim for:

- Disinclination – insurance talk for cold feet, being stood-up, dumped at the altar.
- Dreadful British weather, e.g. mucky grey skies and rain.

Like any other insurance, quotes can be tailored to your own needs. In a nutshell, wedding insurance can cover rescheduling, replacement and reimbursements.

We can't talk insurance without the odd snigger at real-life nightmare claims. How about the bride and groom who filled the church with over 100 twinkling tea-lights, and then watched in horror as the flowers caught fire and the church started to burn? Or the American bride who hired a vintage car to take her to church, and the car's proud owner polished the backseat with red-wax so it would shine? When the bride walked down the aisle, her backside was as red as a baboon's from where all the wax had rubbed off. If you have to put in a claim because the church you're getting married in has been struck by lightning on your wedding day, then perhaps it's someone trying to tell you something!

Boiled chicken, hard veg and lumpy gravy, Sir?

It's probably the most expensive meal of your life, so give your wedding food and drink some serious thought. We've all been to weddings and chewed for hours on boiled chicken and cold, hard veg. You really don't want yours to be one of them.

The world of wedding grub can be another vortex waiting for you to fall into – but there are ways of avoiding the dreadful food crater. First know your budget – whether it's £10 or £50 per head, you'll be able to get something great to feed your guests. Just do the research and ask loads of questions. Remember quality is better than quantity.

If you're on a really tight budget, why not opt to have a KFC bucket wedding breakfast? Jason and Nina Payne got married in Southend and treated their 26 wedding guests to a trip to a local KFC joint for chicken wings, drumsticks, fries and Pepsi. When asked 'why?', Nina said she disliked 'all that poshness' traditionally associated with weddings and Jason said he just 'fancied doing something different'(www.ananova.com). If you don't fancy queuing up in your wedding gear next to the minions for your chicken burger, then why not get the food delivered to your wedding venue? Choose between Family Feast, Variety or a Bargain Bucket, prices start from £9.99–£11.00. Sit back, and watch as your family and friends fight over the chicken legs.

If KFC reminds you a little too much of a night on the lash down the local, rather than your wedding day, then why not call on the services of a celebrity chef? Imagine having your dessert dished-up by Delia, and who better to insult your new mother-in-law than foul-mouthed Gordon Ramsay? Obviously, the cost of a celebrity cook will be hefty, but stuff it! If you want someone like Jamie Oliver at your do, then you're looking at costs of between £15,000–£25,000 for him to attend the event, and that's before he's even picked up a peeler! But, if you have the spend, and are adamant that you want a celebrity then check out www.celebritychefsuk.com or www.limelightentertainment.com

Rosemary Melbourne, from Celebrity Chefs UK, explains what's involved with getting a celebrity to stir-up some fun at your wedding. 'The higher the profile of the chef, the bigger their bill. For a chef who is a household name and instantly recognisable, costs may start at around £6,000 plus for them to attend an event. Then on top of that, you have expenses and other costs, depending on what you want them to do. Most celebrity chefs don't do the cooking, but they will work closely with the caterers to put their stamp on the food served. If you want to avoid the mammoth celebrity bill, then why not consider using a top chef, who isn't as well-known? For example, you could use a good Italian chef who will still cause great excitement amongst your guests, and he will actually cook the food.'

Don't forget the veggies

There are around 60 million people living on our tiny island and over 3 million of them are vegetarians. Roughly speaking that means that 5 percent of people are vegetarians, making it highly likely there will be guests at your wedding who will pass on the offer of chewing something that once had a mother! So why not scrap the meat altogether and go all-out animal friendly?

There are vegetarian caterers out there who will serve up some fantastic nosh without a sniff of a lame vegetable lasagne or soggy mushroom stroganoff. The Vegetarian Society can help www.vegsoc.org

Bubbles and fizz

For most of your guests the drinks served at your wedding are just as important (if not a little more) than the bride's dress. Weddings for many people are about one thing: getting drunk. If you're dreaming of having champagne flowing from the moment you say 'I do' until they turn the lights on, expect to spend a hefty chunk of your budget. Don't feel like you have to serve the real thing. Many sparkling wines and cavas are excellent substitutes – just as long as you choose carefully. These days, there are so many types of fizz at such wildly varying prices; it's hard to know where to start.

Simpleton's Guide to Fizz

- The real stuff is only made in the Champagne region of north-east France. No other sparkling wines can use the treasured 'champagne' name. If you're willing to fork out £25 or more for a fine champagne, you should get a wonderful wine. Spend under £15 and you could end up with something nasty. Better off going for sparkling wine.
- Ozzies, Kiwis and Californians are especially good at making sparkling wine. This is your best option if you want to share some nice bottles of bubbly with a smaller group of people and don't want to fork out for the high-end stuff.
- For a large bash then the answer is easy: choose cava, Spain's traditional sparkling wine. Made in the Penedès region of eastern Spain, cava really is one of the best buys of the wine world. Expect to pay a fiver, or even less, for a really nice bottle.

Check the label:

- *Brut* indicates a very dry wine and is the most like champagne.
- *Sec* indicates a dry wine.
- *Demi-sec* is medium dry.
- *Doux* is sweet.

The biggest trend at the moment is wedding cocktails. Why not tie them into your colour scheme, or personalise the drinks even further and give them names? Lazy Ass's Love Potion, a Bridezilla Buster, Moonie on the Manchester Ship Canal, Romance in Romford or Snogging in Skipton would go down a treat. The best celebrity bashes all have an ice sculpture – with vodka flowing freely from it.

Decide on whether you'll be having a cash bar or free bar. The latter is obviously wide open for violation from greedy drinkers, so be warned!

Want to raise your toast with a free conscience? Then choose wine with real corks. The increasing use of screw-top bottles is causing Spanish and Portuguese farmers to destroy the cork forests that are home to the endangered Iberian lynx.

Have your cake and eat it

Whether you choose the traditional three-tiered fruit cake or the more trendy individual cupcakes, the wedding cake is usually the focal point of the reception and another great opportunity to show off. The average cost of a cake is around £300, but there are loads of options to spend a lot less or a lot more.

You can buy three individual iced fruit cakes from Asda for around £30 (to make a tiered cake) or order one from an experienced cake maker. If you don't like fruit cake, then what about sponge, chocolate or cheesecake? Whatever you go for, personalise it with flowers, feathers, glitter and bows. Or have a laugh, with something a tad different – Posh and Becks had naked icing figures perched on the top of their cake. Or how about making the cake a miniature replica of the top table, and adding marzipan figurines of all the important members of the wedding party? The world of novelty cakes is huge and the ideas are endless.

Whatever you decide on to decorate the cake, just don't do what Jennifer Lopez did at one of her numerous weddings – she had her new husband's name iced-on top of the cake and they spelt it wrong! Obviously, money cannot buy brains. One dyslexic cake decorator, now turned acclaimed artist, had a few run-ins with people after she misspelt several people's names.

If you're really starting to have to count the coppers at the bottom of Mr Pig, then the cake is actually one area that you can scrimp on. You can cover the ropiest of cakes with some fancy icing and make it look splendid.

But how far would you go to save some money on the cake? How about having your cake made in one country, and then having it delivered to where you live via coach? It might sound like something from a Hugh Grant film, but one particular 30-something groom did just that. He loved his mummy's baking so much, he got her to bake it in her kitchen in Ireland, she then gave it to the local coach driver who put it on the seat next to him, and drove the cake all the way to Victoria coach station in London. It arrived in one piece and tasted delicious.

N.B. Just remember to arrange the cake well in advance of the day to avoid any tantrums in the supermarket cake aisle the night before your do!

Entertaining moments

yes!

MARRIAGE IS LIKE A VIOLIN. AFTER THE MUSIC IS OVER, YOU STILL HAVE THE STRINGS.

Anon

Entertainment is one thing you really need to give some serious thought to. You might find Uncle Reg humming the tune to 'My Way' funny, but are you really sure everyone else will? You need something to entertain your guests if you want to avoid food fights and reckless behaviour before 4pm in the afternoon.

But what type of thing do you fancy? Swing or jazz bands are popular and add an air of style to the day; magicians will entertain the kids, but probably cheese everyone else off with their naff tricks. You could opt for a vocalist on a cordless microphone roaming free amongst the guests, singing to anyone that takes their fancy, or, how about a mini-casino?

It would get family and friends bonding, and might even make the odd person flush.

If you want to offer something different then how about a ventriloquist, a comedian or, even better, some Oompa Loompas? Wedding Planner Rebecca Hulme-Edwardson has arranged a wedding where the bride and groom insisted that those little friends of Charlie's attend. 'I worked with one particularly eccentric couple who had a Narnia-meets-*The Secret Garden*-meets-*Alice in Wonderland* wedding, complete with hog-roast garden party. They had someone dressed up as a grizzly bear that went into the wedding during the ceremony, didn't say anything, then just got up and drove away in the groom's car. The bear turned up again later while they were having the first dance, tapped the bride on the shoulder and started to dance with her. They also had Oompa Loompas coming into the reception for a little dance and then leave, without a mention. They wanted to leave all the guests wondering. It was the second wedding for both of them, and they had a budget of £60,000. We had a lot of fun organising it.'

What most wedding guests want, and accept for that matter, is a chance to kick off their shoes and get some moves going on the dance floor. All those truly awful cheesy wedding classics guaranteed to get every woman and the token drunk bloke dancing. When researching your DJ, be sure to ask for a CD with a sample of the music they play. Speak to the DJ directly so you can talk them through exactly what it is you want and highlight what music you don't even want in the building, never mind on the CD player. Shop around to get a good deal and book as early as you can because, as with all other things, the best ones go first.

If you want to avoid cheesy tunes, start thinking about the type of stuff you want played early so you can build up a long list. If you are just having entertainment in the evening, then why not organise the music yourself for the ceremony, the reception and the meal? The average wedding last 11 hours; bands normally play three 45-minute sets and DJs usually work for about four hours, so that's around seven hours of music you need to fill. N.B. 15 songs = approx. 45 minutes, so get scouring that CD collection.

It's always best to make sure that everyone involved with the musical side of your day knows what they should be doing. One particular bride was planning to stroll down the aisle to the tune from *Robin Hood: Prince of Thieves*; except the doddery old organist wasn't sure how it went, so played 'Robin Hood, Robin Hood riding through the glen'. The bride and groom galloped down the aisle!

The first dance

One part of the day that offers everyone immense entertainment is the newlyweds' first dance. The mickey-taking value is great and if it is not handled properly the experience can be mortifying. You either gallop round the dance floor as if on horseback and stamp on each other's toes because you've never danced like that before, or you take to the stage like professionals from *Stricly Come Dancing* and amaze all your mates. Many brides and grooms in the USA go for dance lessons before they say 'I do'. Toby and Lila, from San Diego, got married in summer 2006 and entertained their guests with their first dance to Salt-n-Pepa's 'Push It'. They'd secretly been having Hip-Hop lessons and had learnt a nifty routine. The song got them a standing ovation from guests and even saw some older members of the wedding party trying their hand at some cool moves.

Tammy and Jed, from Auckland, ignored the first dance tradition and hired some traditional Maori dancers to do it for them. Guests got the shock of their lives when 12 Maoris, in traditional dress and men armed with spears, danced the *haka*, while they tucked into their wedding jelly. 'We were both dreading the thought of the first dance so we decided to do something different,' explains Tammy. 'We knew everyone would love the Maori dancers, and it would make our guests remember the day. Everyone loved it.'

When Bazza and Nic, from Melbourne, decided to get married in Hawaii, they flew sixty of their friends and family over to the sunny island of Oahu for a civil ceremony and barbecue on Waikiki Beach. Obviously unable to do the traditional foxtrot or waltz on the sand, they decided to entertain everyone with a spot of Hula Dancing. When the time came for the first dance, Bazza nipped behind a palm tree and changed into a grass skirt. Stupidly he decided to go commando, thinking that no one would know. After lots of bottom-wiggling, finger-clacking and cheering from the wedding guests, the best man rugby-tackled Bazza and pulled down his skirt, revealing his bits to the world, and Nic's rather shocked Gran.

The next thing you really need to get right is what track you want for the first dance song. We've all been to weddings and sniggered into our cake as the bride and groom flounce round the floor to something truly sickly. Remember – you're declaring to everyone who you are through your music – so the track can be lovely, playful or even ironic. It should give you pleasure on your wedding day and long afterwards, not make your mates burst into song whenever it's played in the pub. Think long and hard about what track you want.

My first dance was 'Come Fly with Me' by Frank Sinatra. A couple of seconds into the dance and so-called mates were shouting out, 'Isn't that the theme tune to ITV's *Airport?*' I'll never live it down!

We did a Bridal Moments survey and asked brides and grooms about their thoughts on wedding music:

Classic (if not slightly sickly) first dance songs:

- 'What a Wonderful World' – Louis Armstrong
- 'A Million Love Songs' – Take That
- 'It Had to Be You' – Harry Connick, Jr.
- 'When I Fall in Love' – Frank Sinatra
- 'Some Guys Have All the Luck' – Rod Stewart

- 'I Don't Want to Miss a Thing' – Aerosmith
- 'Always and Forever' – Luther Vandross
- 'She's the One' – Robbie Williams
- 'I've Got You Under My Skin' – Cole Porter
- 'You Do Something to Me' – Paul Weller
- 'I'm Sticking with You' – Velvet Underground
- 'She's Electric' – Oasis
- 'Crazy for You' – Madonna
- 'I Get a Kick Out of You' – Frank Sinatra
- 'Nobody Does It Better' – Carly Simon

No-no first dance songs:

- 'I Will Survive' – Gloria Gaynor
- 'Can't Fight This Feeling' – REO Speedwagon
- 'I'll Do Anything for Love, but I Won't Do That' – Meatloaf
- Any songs by Celine Dion
- 'Ob-La-Di, Ob-La-Da' – The Beatles

Classic drunken last dance songs:

- 'Dizzy' – The Wonder Stuff
- 'I'm a Believer' – The Monkees
- 'I Bet You Look Good on the Dance Floor' – Arctic Monkeys

- 'Groove is in the Heart' – Deee-Lite
- 'Come on Eileen' – Dexy's Midnight Runners
- 'My Way' – Frank Sinatra
- 'Hey Jude' – The Beatles
- 'All You Need is Love' – The Beatles

N.B Always check with the DJ that they have the song you want, otherwise you could end up with the B-side – a cover version by a boyband.

Weddings and technology

Technology has encroached on every other area of our lives, so it's about time it reached the wedding day.

1. **Ditch the DJ and use your iPod.** If you're stressing about paying the price for top entertainment, then stop. How about cutting some corners and putting all your music on an iPod or MP3 player?
   Just create your perfect playlist for the service, reception, meal and evening bash, download all the tracks and, hey presto!, you've got your wedding entertainment. The iPod will need to be connected to a PA system, so you'll probably have to borrow or rent a suitable sound system, including speakers, amplifiers, cables and a microphone. Using an iPod gives you more control over the quality of what's

played and the tone of the day. Ensure you do a sound/technical check to make sure everything works. Dedicate someone with technical fingers to press play.

2. **Broadcast your wedding online.** Since getting engaged, I've harboured a secret thought that I'll soon be getting a call from *Hello!* or *OK!* offering millions for my wedding story. But, as my big sister and self-appointed chief-bridesmaid politely told me, 'get your head out of your backside; you're really not that special.' If, like me, you'd like to share your wedding with the world, then why not broadcast it on the web? It's simple – a laptop, a webcam and some webspace and you're pretty much there. Then you can spread the word to friends and relatives who, whilst unable to attend the actual day, can watch it online. UK firm Network Webcams set up a camera across the street from the Windsor Guildhall when Charles and Camilla got married, so that people all over the world could spot the celebrity faces arriving at the royal wedding. Many registry offices now offer webcams in their rooms.

3. **How about a wedding website?** Not for everyone, but lots of brides and grooms are revelling in the chance to capture their big day online. For the cost of a couple of G&Ts, you can get a basic website and hosting that will enable you to create a place online for all your wedding memorabilia. Check out www.ewedding.com, www.weddingbrand.com and www.weddingorg.com for help on putting your site together.

4. **Online photo albums.** If you don't fancy a wedding website, but still want your photos online, then why not use sites like www.flickr.com to upload all your images? Choose whether you want the world to have access to stare at your mug shots or set it as invite-only. It's a cheap and cheerful wedding photo album.

Wedding games

Why not give your wedding audience a reason to actually listen to the speeches? If you throw in a few wedding games, and bribe them with the promise of a rubbish gift, you're guaranteed some ears bending in your direction.

Wedding bingo

It's dead simple: using words or phrases from your speech, make up enough bingo cards for everyone at the wedding (or if that sounds like too much hard work then do one per table). Eh? For example, if in your speech you will be talking about where you met and where you got engaged, you might use words like:

> Beer, At a party, Boat, Trowel, One-night stand, Across a crowded dance floor, She phoned me, Candyfloss, Virgin Atlantic, Sheffield, Water, Stripper, Fax machine, Hoola Dancing, Yes, yes yes!, Shakespeare, Striped trousers, Flowers, Jaffa Cake, Big pants, Photo frame, Fish & Chip shop, Spoon, Stapler, Sex shop

Don't forget to include some words/phrases that aren't in your speech. There can be only one card with all the correct words.

Wedding quiz

Why not do a wedding quiz? Guests could do it while they're waiting for you to come back from having the photos taken, or maybe after dinner before the evening guests arrive.

Put together some questions about you and your new husband, and make the questions easy enough so most people will know the answer. Some examples:

Where did the Bridezilla and Lazy Ass meet?

A.   In a launderette.

B.   At 1.55am at a works party when they were looking for a late night snog.

C.   On their friend's boat.

Do the newlyweds intend to start trying for a family now they are married?

A.   Yes, right after they've cut the cake...

B.   No, they still have a lot of the world to see.

C.   Yes, they want to have enough kids for their own football team.

Who was it out of Bridezilla and Lazy Ass who drank urine by mistake when they were 14?

A.   It's got to be Lazy Ass, he'd drink anything.

B.   It was Bridezilla, I was standing next to her when she took a gulp.

C.   Neither of them, they only ever drink alcohol.

Who was it that broke their wrist picking daffodils when they were drunk?

A.   Bridezilla, she loves fresh flowers.

B.   Lazy Ass, that's why he's got such a limp wrist.

C.   Sounds like something Lazy Ass would do to impress the ladies.

Wedding word search

A wedding word search is a good way of keeping little
people quiet for a while.

b	r	i	d	e	s	m	a	i	d
f	l	o	w	e	r	s	e	r	h
a	p	g	r	o	o	m	n	b	v
v	a	v	f	b	d	g	y	w	e
o	r	a	q	r	n	c	a	v	i
u	t	c	v	i	u	a	p	s	l
r	y	o	d	d	y	k	m	g	x
s	h	d	k	e	j	e	a	n	p
b	e	e	b	l	u	e	h	i	j
w	i	n	v	i	t	e	c	r	u

Flowers, Blue, Groom, Bride, Cake, DJ, Invite, Champagne,
Veil, Rings, Wedding, Party, Bridesmaid Favours

Wedding holidays

BY ALL MEANS MARRY;

IF YOU GET A GOOD WIFE,

YOU'LL BE HAPPY; IF YOU

GET A BAD ONE, YOU'LL

BECOME A PHILOSOPHER.

Socrates

Hens and stags

Hen, stag, bachelor or bachelorette parties, or whatever name you give them, they are usually nights, weekends or even weeks of drunken naughtiness and mischief. The more traditional types usually include endless boob flashing, moonies, ladies clad in headdresses littered with L-plates, men dressed as gimps, eyebrow shaving, hair-dyeing, and strippers.

Or, there's the more slightly sedate type that many people are veering towards, like a golfing weekend in Scotland, an adventure sports weekend away, a mature cocktail party or a relaxing trip to a health spa in Switzerland.

Whatever you do, wherever you go, these will result in many moments to remember. Some you'll talk about and others you won't!

Apparently Spain is the most popular foreign destination for stag parties and hen bashes, followed by the Netherlands and France.

Organise it yourself, hand the responsibility to a trusted sibling or mate, or call in the experts. There are different organisations that can help. For some great ideas, look at:

www.thestagandhengroup.co.uk
www.brilliantweekends.co.uk

We've cobbled together some suggestions to set your brain whirring.

Ideas for hens

- Dreamt of being served cocktails by your very own waiter – then why not call on the Butlers in the Buff? The perfect accessory for a hen party, they serve you drinks, canapés and just generally wander round the venue wearing very little and looking very cheeky! Stacey, from Butlers in the Buff, explains why they are becoming so popular. 'All our butlers are hand-picked. They are handsome, good-looking men, who make a refreshing change from the sleazy strippers usually associated with hen parties. They can serve you cocktails, act as host for the first few hours of the party and just generally bring a spot of fun and cheekiness to any event. It's just innocent fun, but we ask that ladies be gentle with the butlers!' Have a peek at them for yourself, visit www.butlersinthebuff.co.uk

- A long weekend in Prague, Barcelona or Paris, starting with a spot of culture, then on to shopping, cocktails and a fantastic meal, then dancing.
- Pole-dancing lessons, followed by normal dancing and lots of wine.
- A weekend at the races including a glam day betting on the horses, followed by a night on the town. The next day detox and unwind with treats in a spa.
- A murder mystery weekend. Spend the weekend playing Miss Marple, with tea and scones, the odd sherry and trying to figure out 'Who did it?' Was it Professor Plum in the library?
- Book a pamper party – either before you go off for your do or when you come back, to help relax and detox. Check out www.pamperparty.co.uk
- Spend the weekend chucking tomatoes during the Tomatina festival in Valencia, Spain. Around

250,000lbs of tomatoes get thrown in what has to be the world's biggest food fight.

- Get crafty; spend the weekend painting or perfecting your pottery. Get your mates to make something for you as a keepsake.
- Don a yellow coat and go all *Hi-De-Hi* with a trip to Butlins or Pontins.

Ideas for stags

- Rock climbing in Fontainebleau, France.
- Guns and Wheels Weekend, including paint-balling and quad biking, followed by a meal in Hooters, then onto a comedy club or lap dancing club. Visit www.designaventure.co.uk
- A weekend in Estonia, including wild boar hunting.
- A trip to Budapest including 4x4 woodland safari, driving a mini-monster digger and medieval banquet.
- A weekend in Ibiza, on the beach by the day and clubbing by night.
- An adventure weekend in the UK: go-karting and clay pigeon shooting, followed by a big barbecue, then a night on the beer. The following day, abseiling with a raging hangover.

- Go in search of the Loch Ness Monster. Get the train to Loch Ness and go on a pub crawl in search of Nessy. Have haggis for breakfast, buy a tartan skirt and have a go at tossing the caber.
- What about a weekend by the sea? Choose either Blackpool or Brighton for fish and chips, slot machines, warm beer and footy on the big screen, and then spend the evening in a casino.

Honeymoon

Why the Honeymoon?

In ancient times, many of the first marriages were by capture, not choice. When early man felt it was time to take a bride, he would often carry off an unwilling woman to a secret place where her relatives wouldn't find them. While the moon went through all its phases (about 30 days), they hid from the searchers and drank a brew made from honey. Hence, we get the word, honeymoon.

The second wedding holiday – Lazy Ass should really be smiling now.

Ask anyone who has ever got married and they'll tell you that after all the organising, and build-up to the big day, the point they look forward to reaching most is the postnuptial voyage. When they disappear into the sunset for quality time with their newly-crowned husband or wife, for some time spent under the duvet, lazing around, and drinking stupidly big cocktails. But what you do, where you go and how much you spend on the trip, is a personal thing and depends on taste, time and budget. Once again there is the added pressure to make this the holiday-of-a-lifetime, but with a little bit of thinking and planning there's no reason it can't be.

Mintel calculates that spending on honeymoons abroad is currently worth between £500–£600 million a year, a figure that has doubled since 1998. According to a recent survey, couples spend an average £2,963 on their honeymoon, up £106 on the previous year. They also splash out an average £205 on a hotel for the first night.

So whereas our parents might have scraped together enough money for a week in Bournemouth in a B&B, or a long weekend in Paris, for noughties newlyweds the world is your oyster. But, before you reach for those glossy honeymoon brochures that promise golden sands and crystal clear waters in Maldives or perhaps Mauritius, think about what you really want to do and where you really want to go.

What would really get your blood pumping? How about ditching the wheelie suitcase, matching vanity case and 5-star hotel, for a rucksack and two weeks backpacking round China and Vietnam? What about two weeks detoxing in an Australian Eco-lodge perfect for vegetarian yoga lovers, a trek to Peru in search of the Incas, or a safari to South Africa to get up close and personal with the wild animals? Scan your eyes over our honeymoon checklist which should get you doing some holiday soul-searching. Highlight the things that interest you.

Checklist items:

- Hot or cold weather
- Beaches
- Mountains
- Vineyards
- Cruise ship
- City
- Off the beaten track
- Hiking
- Biking
- Boat rental
- Tennis
- Golf
- Swimming
- Sunbathing

- Diving
- Snorkeling
- Guided tours
- Museums
- Theatre
- Skiing
- Large resort
- B&B
- Hotel room with balcony
- Ocean-view room
- Couples-only lodging
- Private jacuzzi
- Luxury accommodation
- Room service
- Hotel bar
- All inclusive
- Casual dining
- Formal dining
- Regional/local cuisine

The Mintel survey also discovered that 73 percent of couples choose their honeymoon together, while only 18 percent opt for the tradition of leaving the honeymoon arrangements up to the groom. If you're struggling to agree on where to fly off to, then try the Turquoise Holiday Company (www.turquoiseholidays.co.uk) who can help soothe the headache if Lazy Ass wants to go on a safari, while you're fighting for a beach, a posh hotel and sometime in a spa (www.mintel.co.uk).

Planet-friendly honeymoons

The average passenger leaving a flight from Gatwick Airport is responsible for the equivalent of 85-kilo bags of soot being thrown out of the aeroplane window. A plane carrying 200 passengers would produce some 17,000 bags of soot. Makes you think twice about jumping on that plane, doesn't it? If you want a honeymoon that won't leave a dirty mark on the environment, then contact www.responsible-travel.com or www.ecotourdirectory.com. For a real green honeymoon instead of jetting off to faraway lands, keep your travel to a minimum and stay closer to home. Why not consider a working honeymoon where you can contribute to an environmental project, or raise money for a charity?

A wedding list with a difference

If you fancy flying off somewhere exotic, why not set up a honeymoon-gift list service? You can either ask guests to chip in for the actual cost of the holiday or ask them to buy you specific things you can do while on your trip. Think about it – a new kettle or a trip to Kenya? How about a night in a 7-star hotel on your trip to Dubai; a two-day boat trip on the Amazon during your holiday to Brazil; hang-gliding lessons while you're in Australia; or swimming with dolphins on a honeymoon to Florida? Rainbow Tours (www.rainbowtours.co.uk), and Travel Counsellors (www.travelcounsellors.com/bridalRegistry.aspx) can assist with the logistics of organising a honeymoon-gift list.

The after life

DURING THE FIRST YEAR OF THE WEDDING, PUT A QUID IN A JAR EACH TIME YOU MAKE LOVE. THEN DURING THE SECOND YEAR, TAKE A QUID OUT EACH TIME YOU MAKE LOVE. AT THE END OF THE SECOND YEAR, GO TO A GOOD RESTAURANT WITH WHAT'S LEFT...

So, your wedding journey is drawing to a close. You're either just back off your honeymoon all tanned and looking forward to married life. Or you're still tapping your single toes waiting for the big day to arrive, and couldn't resist finding out what the last chapter of the book says about the after life.

Post-nuptial blues

After all the flitting about organising the wedding day and the wonders and romance of the honeymoon, it's not surprising that when the wedding bubble bursts and you land back in your living-room, it can be an anti-climax. For some poor brides their depression totally takes hold and they end up with what psychologists call 'Post-nuptial blues'.

Post-wedding perks

1. Plan something nice for when you return from honeymoon: a night on the town with your mates, a dinner party, or just your favourite bottle of wine, a DVD and the sofa.
2. The chances are you've got all your wedding presents to play with. So enjoy them while they are still new. Don't forget to write thank you cards – it's good karma.

3. Relish having your life back and not having to spend every weekend traipsing round bridal fairs, shops and florists. Go into a furniture store, go and buy loads of CDs or how about a new TV?
4. Decorate your bedroom – turn it into a sexy boudoir.
5. Move house.
6. Have a baby.
7. Change career.
8. Learn a language.
9. Even better, buy a house abroad.
10. Go into a newsagent, ignore the wedding glossies, and buy another magazine instead.

What do you expect from marriage?

On the following pages are list of statements that are related to marriage – circle the ones that relate to what you think marriage means and what you want from your new relationship.

We'll be more grown-up.

We'll always be together.

The fruit bowl will
always be full.

Our commitment is real.

It'll be nice to share the
same name and be a
proper family.

We'll always be happy.

She'll learn how to
arrange flowers I spend a
blooming fortune on.

He'll always put the loo
seat down.

We will no longer have
to sleep under the dining
table when we visit his
parents. We'll get one
of the double beds.

It will be harder to
split up.

I'll finally be able
to cook.

My underwear no longer
has to match.

As a husband he will
instantly know how to
put a shelf up and bleed a
radiator.

She'll finally buy her
own razor.

I'll no longer kill all
plants that I come into
contact with.

We'll share the good
times and the bad.

We'll always have
great sex.

As a wife she will learn
how to leave me alone
when I'm watching
the footy.

The bathroom will
always be clean because
wives don't like poohing
in a mucky place.

We'll provide a stable
home to bring up kids.

Sunday morning is for
making love, breakfast
in bed and the weekend
papers.

We'll never run out of
toilet paper again and
have to use kitchen roll
instead.

There will always be
someone to laugh with/at.

I can wear my boxer
shorts for four
consecutive days and
she can't moan, because
she's my wife.

We can finally have the
Christmas Day we want!

We'll no longer leave wet
clothes in the washing
machine for a week.

We won't need our
friends as much.

It makes me feel all warm
and swishy inside.

I can wear those
pyjamas I've been
wanting for ages.

I'm guaranteed a cuddle
after a crappy day.

Back to school exercise: Now make a wish list for your marriage. Write the statements you've circled onto a piece of coloured paper and decorate the page and make a poster. Now stick it on the fridge so you can see it every day. People may mock your artwork and the poster, but it is only because they're jealous.

A husband is living proof that a wife can take a joke.

Does marriage change your relationship?

So after the balloons have deflated and the wedding gifts have been unpacked, oohed! at, and then dumped in the sink with last night's curry crusted to them – then what? As newlyweds, does that automatically mean you will spend the rest of your natural life feeding each other grapes, drinking wine from gold goblets and never letting go of each other? Well, probably not.

If you lived over the brush before walking down the aisle, then you're probably thinking that nothing much is going to change now your Mr & Mrs/Ms. Well, apart from maybe your name, and the contents of your jewellery box. But think again, because apparently according to relationship experts, things can change. Christine Northam, from Relate, shares her in-depth knowledge of newlyweds. 'If you've lived together before getting married, then you'll have a good idea what to expect when you come back from honeymoon. But don't be fooled into thinking that everything will stay the same, because for many couples things do change. You've made a public commitment, so your relationship is more official, and there can be more pressure to make it succeed. With every change there is a sense of loss. You're no longer a carefree couple any more, people will be looking at you through different eyes. Talk about how you feel about this new stage in your relationship. It's an exciting time.'

Co-habitors on being married

'Marriage did change our relationship. We're more settled and are thinking about starting a family.'

Lesley

'Saying "I do" didn't make much difference. We had more sex for a while, but then we just went back to doing it once a month.'

Phil

'My mother-in-law phones me for a chat now. She never did that before I married her son.'

Clara

'I'd be lying if I said it I didn't feel different when we first came back from honeymoon. Everything was exciting again. We both used to rush home from work and eat dinner at the table together. But it only lasted a few weeks. Then it was back to normal, tea on a tray in front of the TV.'

Tim

'We didn't change, but other people changed towards us. It was as if they expected us to grow up overnight and suddenly become responsible. But that isn't going to happen.'

Andy

'It makes me work harder to solve any problems that pop up.'

Noel

'I feel closer to him and like saying the words "my husband" when I talk about him.'

Heather

New York Reverend Laurie Sue Brockway agrees that relationships do change when you say 'I do' and offers her hand-picked hints for starting off on the right foot:

1. Continue dating.
2. Continue talking and communicating.
3. Make your bedroom a sacred space free from complaints and anger.
4. Tell each other what you love about each other regularly.
5. When you want to reconnect, repeat your wedding vows at bedtime.

When a newly-married man looks happy, we know why. But when a ten-year-married man looks happy, we wonder why.

The new anniversary laws

Whereas before you were married you celebrated a made-up anniversary, like the first time you met, the first kiss or whatever. Now you're married grown-ups, you have proper anniversaries just like your mum and dad. Even better, each anniversary comes with its own theme, so you know what kind of present to buy as the years roll by.

	British	American	Modern
1	Cotton	Paper	Clocks
2	Paper	Cotton	China
3	Leather	Leather	Crystal
4	Linen, silk	Fruit, flowers	Appliances
5	Wood	Wood	Silverware
6	Sugar	Iron	Wooden
7	Wool, copper	Wool, copper	Desk item
8	Bronze, pottery	Bronze	Linens, lace
9	Pottery, willow	Pottery	Leather
10	Tin	Tin, aluminium	Diamond jewellery
11	Steel	Steel	Jewellery
12	Linen	Silk	Pearls
13	Lace	Lace	Textiles, fur
14	Ivory	Ivory	Gold
15	Crystal	Crystal	Watches
20	Chinaware	Chinaware	Platinum
25	Silver	Silver	Sterling silver
30	Pearl	Pearl	Diamond
35	Coral	Coral, jade	Jade
40	Ruby		
45	Sapphire		
50	Gold		
55	Emerald		
60	Diamond		
65	Blue Sapphire		
70	Platinum		
75	Diamond		
80	Oak		

It seems a lot better to follow the traditional anniversary themes than the modern – who on earth wants a 'desk item' for their seventh anniversary?

No one seems to know the reason, but after you've celebrated your 15th anniversary with a lovely piece of crystal, advice on what you're supposed to get disappears until your 20th anniversary. So we've put together a few suggestions that you can choose from:

Shoes	Chocolate
Season ticket	Kate Spade bag
Ticket for the World Cup	iTunes vouchers
Rugby	Curry
Gardening	Silence
Champagne	Ale
Cake	Binoculars
Egg and chips	Red underwear
Lycra	Cheap flight
Basket of fruit and veg	Tea and biscuits

Married life is full of excitement and frustration:

- In the first year of marriage, the man speaks and the woman listens.
- In the second year, the woman speaks and the man listens.
- In the third year, they both speak and the neighbours listen.

Happy ever after

So there you have it. We've travelled the full length of the wedding boulevard together and arrived safely. Along the way, I've pointed out a few black holes that were lurking in the shadows and suggested ways of coping with overzealous relatives. I've given you hints on how to prize Lazy Ass's backside off the sofa; tips on coping with those bridal tantrums; and how to find the dream honeymoon destination.

You now have all my wedding wisdom, and we hope you put it to good use and get the day you dreamed of, or as close as you possibly can. I wish you a really great marriage, filled with lots of laugher, larking around, and love.

Life on the other side isn't that much different. I still have to fight to get in the bathroom in the morning and, worst of all, listen to the incessant drone of sports commentators on the radio when I travel in my husband's car. Seven months on and we still childishly snigger when we're referred to as husband or wife, but we're slowly growing up.

Now the wedding is done and dusted. In true female style, I'm looking for the next thing to get obsessed about. How about having a baby?

The last words in the book really should go to the people who have been married for over 30 years, and still manage to smile at each other over the breakfast table and kiss each other good night. With or without their teeth!

The secret to a long and happy marriage

'ALWAYS *have the last word in an argument –* *sorry dear.'*

Andrew, Canberra, Australia

'A *vital ingredient for a happy marriage is a compatible sense of humour. Nothing brings and keeps you closer together than a laugh.'*

Lynda, Cardiff

'Put up *with each other's moans and groans all the time and sling a deaf ear.'*

Pete, Manchester

'*Give and take.*'

Brian, Arizona

'*Have lots of patience – and listen to each other.*'

Edna, Manchester

In June 2005, Percy and Florence Arrowsmith made it into the Guinness World Records for the world's longest marriage of 80 years. The couple also held the record for being the oldest married couple in the world until Percy died.

'*It is all about hard work. We have had our arguments but we work through them together. We always go to bed as friends and always make up before we go to sleep with a kiss and a cuddle.*'

Florence

'*Saying yes, dear.*'

Percy

'*If you want a lasting relationship then buy a dog!*'

Bill, London

REFERENCES, BIBLIOGRAPHY

AND LIST OF WEBSITES

Bridal Moments bibliography

Blayney, Molly Dolan, *Wedded Bliss: A Victorian Bride's Handbook* (Abbeville Press, 1992)

Brockway, Rev. Laurie Sue, *Wedding Goddess: A Divine Guide To Transforming Wedding Stress into Wedding Bliss* (Perigee Books, 2005)

Exley, Helen, *Marriage It Drives Us Crazy* (Exley Publications, 2004)

Kingsland, Burton, *Etiquette for All Occasions* (Doubleday, 1901)

Websites used for research, and worth visiting:

www.almostnewweddingdresses.co.uk
www.ananova.com
www.brilliantweekends.co.uk
www.carbonplanet.com
www.celebritychefsuk.com

www.confetti.co.uk
www.designaventure.co.uk
www.ebay.com
www.ecotourdirectory.com
www.elegancebridalstudio.co.uk
www.ewedding.com
www.flickr.com
www.groomservice.co.uk
www.hitched.co.uk
www.itunes.co.uk
www.limelightentertainment.com
www.mintel.co.uk
www.netbrides.com
www.organicweddings.com
www.oxfam.org.uk
www.quotationspage.com
www.rainbowtours.co.uk
www.relate.org.uk
www.responsibletravel.com
www.statistics.gov.uk
www.thecarbonneutralcompany.co.uk
www.thedressmarket.com
www.thestagandhengroup.co.uk
www.theweddingandpartyplanner.co.uk
www.threadheadcreations.com
www.travelcounsellors.com/bridalRegistry.aspx
www.ukawp.co.uk
www.ukdps.co.uk
www.vegsoc.org
www.weddingbrand.com
www.weddinggoddess.com
www.weddingorg.com
www.wedding-references.com
www.weddingwardrobe.co.uk
www.wholly-jo.co.uk
www.youandyourwedding.co.uk

ACKNOWLEDGEMENTS

Writing this book allowed me to immerse myself in the world of weddings and helped me to dodge several scary wedding moments of my own. I got to ask lots of people annoying questions about their big day – causing everyone around me to think I was truly paranoid and neurotic about getting hitched. A big thanks to Brendan M. for the opportunity to write this book and to Marshall Cavendish for making it happen.

To everyone who came to my wedding, I hope you enjoyed it. Thanks to Mum and Dad, who've supported me in absolutely everything I've ever wanted to do – no matter how hair-brained. To the 'in-laws' for letting me join your family (even though I'm rubbish at sport and don't like rugby). Big kisses to the fabulous big and little bridesmaids, and to all the wedding blokes; especially the little ones with the cameras.

A big thanks to everyone who let me write about their wedding screw-ups – I've changed the names of a few to save them from the humiliation. And to Gram, who would have loved to have read this book.

The last word has to go to my very own Lazy Ass, aka, my fabulous hairy husband, Reedy or rather Jonathan Andrew Reed, who did diddlysquat towards our wedding apart from fend off bad bouts of bridal mania and provide just the right amount of G&Ts. Long may the adventures and mischief continue.

And to little Rory, the most handsome and funniest little boy ever to be born.

SPECIAL THANKS

I would like to say a huge thank you to all the people who allowed me to interview them and publish their words of wisdom:

The Reverend Laurie Sue Brockway
Christine Northam, Relate counsellor
Professor Ben Fletcher, Head of Psychology at the
    University of Hertfordshire
Kate Webster, owner of Lace Bridal Store, Hale, Cheshire
Matt Hepplestone, owner of Red Floral Architecture,
    Stalybridge, Cheshire
Michael Peckett, Hairdresser, Cheshire
Andy Newman, Wedding Insurance Expert
Rosemary Melbourne, Celebrity Chefs UK
Kate Hipkins, Pronuptia
Stacey Lynn, Butlers in the Buff
Rebecca Hulme-Edwardson, The Wedding and
    Party Planner, Nottingham
Laura Balance, Playland

ABOUT THE AUTHOR

Helen Dugdale has always wanted to be a writer and, at the tender age of eight, wrote and illustrated her first book called *Princess and the Tarts* – a story about a princess and her burnt jam tarts.

She has developed a successful career working as a journalist and PR consultant, and now runs her own creative agency, Scribble.

Helen is currently writing a children's book, which will hopefully be on a shelf near you soon.

She was born in Manchester and, having lived and worked in various cities across the UK and in Vancouver, Canada, she is now back in her home town.

She is married to Jonathan and has a young son, Rory.

Helen likes asking lots of questions, shopping and drinking fizz.